LOVE, BLACK LOVE

George Davis
LOVE, BLACK LOVE

ANCHOR PRESS/DOUBLEDAY
GARDEN CITY, NEW YORK
1978

The Anchor Press edition is the first publication
of *Love, Black Love*.

Selections of the book have appeared in *Essence*
Magazine.

ISBN: 0-385-09788-3
Library of Congress Catalog Card Number 74–33636
Copyright © 1977, 1978 by George Davis

George Davis was born in West Virginia. He is a graduate of Colgate University and holds an M.F.A. from Columbia University. He has been a reporter for the Washington *Post* and a deskman for the New York *Times*. He presently teaches at Bronx Community College. His fiction and articles have appeared in dozens of magazines and newspapers, and his first novel, COMING HOME, was published by Random House.

To my mother and father,
Winnie and Clarence Davis,
with love, and to Mary,
Pamela, and George
Christopher.

Contents

Introduction

What is love? How long does it last? Is it light enough to play with? Is it serious enough to drive you crazy? Is it fun? Is it useful? If it fails the first time do you want it to come again? Can you love, really love, two people at once? Or three? Does money make the heart grow fonder?

We know what dictionaries and textbooks say it should be, but that doesn't have a great deal to do with the way people live. This book is about the way people live. The love stories here are based on the intimate revelations of a few of the hundreds of people I interviewed to get opinions on the kinds of questions listed above.

Many of the details in these stories have been fictionalized to insure a degree of anonymity, and each story has been shaped to contain more of the elements of a narrative than of a question-and-answer interview.

Doing the interviewing and putting the book together was fun, if that's the right word. Interesting, fascinating. It is a part of a vast effort on my part to know and write as honestly as I can about what goes on in people's everyday lives. The things that people had to say about love were funny sometimes and touching sometimes, and I am grateful to them for giving honest and revealing accounts of how love is treating them now, at this point, three quarters of the way through this rushing century.

Most of the people in this book are black. As my friend Mervyn Taylor likes to say, love among black people "is love in a narrow space. For us," he says, "love is not a matter of pledging troth beneath the sky and walking off into the sunset to live happily ever after.

"It may involve a brief meeting in a darkened room somewhere, or coming down a stairs and parting, each to go his or her own way. Often it's a matter of making do, of stealing sweetness from the night, with no illusions about permanence."

It is love under the kind of pressure that exposes marrow; thus in these lives we see some of what we all are behind the façades that less urgent circumstances allow us to live behind. Fay Wilson, a friend who came to New York from the West Indies, says that Americans in general are crazy; the people I chose for this book are crazier than most. "They are like characters in a soap opera," she says as she types the manuscript, alternately laughing and frowning at the things the people do trying to be in love.

I swore to her that the stories, though changed, are essentially true. In love you find the oddest combinations: Materialistic people find themselves in love with idealists. Clingers fall in love with players; the deep and intense get hooked on the fly and superficially; homebodies capture and try to smother butterflies. If it weren't so serious we could laugh at it. For example, one young lady, a very happy, pleasant, optimistic young lady, fell in love with a dude so negative that his aura killed all the house plants in her apartment.

"Damn! Dam-m-m-mn!" Mervyn laughed when I told him. He said he knew some negative people, but that beat everything he had ever heard. "Killed the house plants, huh? Damn! Damn! She had to get rid of that dude, huh?"

"Not yet," I said.

"How long have they been together?"

"Seven years."

Another young lady loved only pretty men. That was what she wanted to do with the one life she had: take care of one pretty man after another. "Look at them, enjoy looking at them, I do."

People's motivations can take them to some strange places.

There are a million reasons why people fall in love. Look around you. Watch them. One night I came out of a friend's apartment, where a group of us had been rapping about this. I remember, it was a cold night. February's wind howled down the Grand Concourse, that strange, eight-to-fourteen-lane roadway that cuts through the center of the Bronx.

That night, one young lady had said, "I'd really like to get inside a lot of different kinds of love affairs and check them out, not participate in them—the one I got is enough problem for me—but I'd like to get close enough to some others just to see."

I could understand how she felt. I had similar urges. The seven of us had been talking for a long time. Another woman had said, "I feel that the only kind of love I've ever seen is the kind that runs away when I get close. Why are men so timid?"

I wanted to answer her. I started to say aloud that I was timid, but I didn't say it. I decided to lay back. I started to tell her that I, like most men, don't like to put my feelings on the line, no-o-o, not here in this world.

The young man on the floor said, "I don't want any kind. I don't mess with the stuff myself. The only thing I love is fried chicken and red Kool-Aid." He laughed. His wife, a serious-minded woman, pushed his head down and laughed with him, but she assured us, "He ain't lying." Her face went sad for a moment, and she didn't say much after that.

That's not all that happened that evening, but that's what I most recalled outside in the cold, walking along side the deserted lanes of the Concourse, where, now, at 3 A.M., not even a cab stirred. The faces of the grand old buildings were ashen in the February cold.

I recalled the face of the woman whose husband didn't believe in love. I didn't know who to be sad for, her or him or no one. Each darkened building seemed to hide the same potential for incompatibility. It is what we've learned to live with. No doubt there was a person lying up inside one of those apartments who had received so much love that he failed to appreciate it, and beside him was another person, who had received so little that she feared it whenever it came. Some people up there loved with no chance of being loved in return; others were loved with no thought of loving.

There were teen-agers up there, rolling around unable to sleep for dreaming of it, and religious souls who feared the coming of hell-fire if they gave in to their tormenting urges. Others were alone and didn't give a damn.

There must have been a person on the right side of the Concourse perfectly fitted for someone on the left, but there were dozens of reasons why they would never get together, and hundreds of reasons why they might never stay together if they did. And then there were people up there who really, really loved each other, but these were exceptions.

I have heard psychologists say that it goes back to the way we were raised, to our American childhood; but even if we accept this it doesn't make it easier for us to raise our own children any better. If we bring them up with lots of love they'll come into adulthood trying to love people who've been brought up with none, and even if we give ours love there is no assurance they'll know how to do more than receive it.

When love is good it can make you fly. Winning it is worth the risk. People fall in love and glow for weeks. Some hum like saints who've talked to Jesus. Strange, the things it makes us do.

Not sex. The sexual revolution is not the war that needs to be waged. Figuring out the purely sexual part of the relationship seemed the easy part for most of the people I talked to. The tough problem was getting close, close enough to trust each other, to believe, to understand, to forgive, to love. The sexual revolution has been taken over by technocrats who apparently believe that victory simply waits on the application of the right technology and technique: suck a little bit here, blow a little bit there, improve this piece of equipment, and the war will be over.

In all, there is so little mention of the paradoxes involved when two whole, tense, full, complexed persons get close to each other! The real concern of the people I talked to was with relationships, not with sex per se. So my interest flowed to-

4   *Introduction*

ward those large, mainly tragic stories that good fiction deals with: relationships, and how the problems involved must constantly be illuminated but can never be "solved," unless, of course, we find some way to stop being whole, tense, full, complexed persons.

These stories, then, are attempts to say again what it means to be people. They are reilluminations of the persistence of jealousy, greed, deception, and tenderness.

"I think you like crazy people," Fay said; "people with problems."

"Well, I simply picked people who had something intense and interesting to say about love," I told her.

"Weirdos," she said under her breath, and laughed.

We, black Americans (all exceptions admitted), with our fragile egos and large expectations, love love. We curse and cut each other more often, but we own more "I love you sho-be-do" phonograph records than any other people of twice our number on this planet.

We sit up all night listening to "loving you is easier than breathing." Some of us grew up in houses where the beat and the message were repeated from get-up in the morning to lie-down at night. I can remember that it was sometimes the same record, over and over—"Stay, darling, stay in my corner."

We wouldn't buy a car without a radio. It may not have a back window or treaded tires, but it must have a radio. We walk the streets with transistors plugged into our ears with somebody crooning reassuringly, "Love is the answer" or "Love lifted me this morning."

We have absorbed every popular true and false notion about love, and it is the way that these very ingrained notions collide with the very real facts of our existence that forms the basis of our agony and ecstasy. Other people sing about flowers, or rain, or surfing. We always sing about love. We believe in it, as the faithful believe in salvation. And how we wallow and withdraw when it doesn't save, but, oh, how we strut when it does, even for a moment, "for a sugar-, sugar-, sugar-, yea, yea, yea, yea, coated moment," as the record says.

"Most of this is not coated with sugar," Fay said as she finished typing the manuscript.

"Well, okay, you're right," I said.

"Most of it is sad, and some of the people are foolish."

"You're not supposed to judge them, Fay," I said in a last effort to exonerate myself. "You're just supposed to decide if any of the truth they speak applies to you." I was in one of my rare speech-making moods. Most often, I make speeches only inside my head, but this time I said out loud, "Most love stories are sad, eventually, in real life. And the poignancy that makes a story worth telling is almost always linked in some way to sadness but grandeur, too, because, despite the sadness, we do continue to try."

1
A Love Affair

I think that love can last a lifetime.

I live with a woman I love. Nobody's perfect. I don't think there is such a thing as a perfect relationship, but I love her even though we don't always see eye to eye, and I know that she loves me, in her own way. We've been married for ten years and have three children. The oldest is almost nine, and then we have one seven and one six. I don't think we'll have any more.

Me and my wife have been through a lot together. That's what I think love is, going through whatever you have to go through together. Times are good now, so you can't really prove that much by what happens now. I have a good job as a equipment installation supervisor for a private telephone company. Without overtime, I make over fifteen thousand dollars a year.

I don't work on equipment myself unless it is a big system. Otherwise, I send out a crew. Most of the men who work for us—black and white—aren't worth a damn. I have to knock heads to get the work done, but basically I have a good job.

My family lives well, and I come out and have a beer a couple nights a week. Because you see me out here, that don't mean I'm running around. I get bored at home, that's true, but what I like to do is work on my car or come out and have a beer and talk to the guys you saw me with.

Earl, he's married and he had a outside woman. I would too if I had a wife like his. If you got a good woman you don't need a outside woman, because if your wife finds out about it that's going to mess up the good thing that you got at home.

The main thing right now is that my wife is easy to live with. She don't raise no hell. She don't waste money, and she's a great mother for the kids. Half of these women I see out here I wouldn't want over top of my kids.

But there are different levels of love. You love more when you're first married, and then it changes to another kind of love as you go along. I mean, you can't expect it to stay the same, but if times got bad that would prove if it's still love. I think me and my wife had a sweeter love when times were bad: when I was in the service making private's pay.

I remember the time when we had one can of sardines to

eat. I didn't want to eat it, because she was pregnant and I wanted her to have it, and she didn't want to eat it, because I had to go out in the field in the cold and she wanted me to have it. No furniture. We sat on the floor and played pitty-pat and whoever lost would have to eat the sardines—whoever *lost*.

I lost but I wouldn't eat them. We slept in my army sleeping bag on the floor listening to the radio. We loved each other very much. She was only seventeen. We didn't know what we was doing. I was stationed in Fort Knox, Kentucky, as a radio operator in a armored battalion.

We didn't have a car, so I hitched back and forth from where we lived, in Louisville, Kentucky, to Fort Knox, which was thirty-four miles away. We were in the field sometimes for weeks in the dead of winter. She was in the apartment alone—no friends, no money, half the time no food, pregnant.

We went through things like that together. When I look back on it, I have to love that woman. I kept telling her that she should go home. Her parents had a big house in Pumphrey, Maryland. She could have stayed with her parents till I got out of the service, but she wanted to be with me. That's one thing about her: she's stubborn. She wouldn't go, man. She wanted us to be together.

We had our baby in Kentucky. The church we went to— the people in the church would loan us a piece of furniture like that, until we had enough to live on. That's what's different about the South. Anything extra that a person has they'll give it to another person or loan it to them. If you find that happening up North you show me where the place is, because I've never seen it.

I'm not trying to put my wife up as a perfect woman. For one thing, she's stubborn as hell, but it's mostly stubborn about me and the kids. She does things like stand in front of the door and won't let me out the door if I don't have my gloves on or something like that. I say, "Maria, I'm working inside. The car is in the garage. I park in the garage at work. I'm not going to be outside."

But she won't move. She won't fuss. She very seldom raises

her voice. I could go out the back door if I wanted to, but I go and get the gloves and leave them on the seat of my car anyway.

She's cute. I don't like a skinny woman, and people in my family have always liked dark-skinned women with big behinds. I would say that she is brown-skinned, though. She's a little bit lighter than me. Some people say you get bored with one woman for ten years, which is true, but in ten years I've never been with another woman.

You think that's a lie, don't you? You think I'm lying. But why would I lie? I don't know you. I'm not trying to impress you as being a perfect man, myself. I'm only saying that in ten years I've never been with another woman.

Sure, marriage is hard. You go to work. You come home tired. You get in a rut, but I wear this ring on my finger and I'll tell a woman quick that I'm a happy married man.

Women tease you all the time; not saying that I'm cute or anything like that, but I look good in my clothes. So a woman might come up to you and say, "You can come and put your shoes under my bed anytime you want to." I laugh and joke with them. I tell them I'm too much man for them to handle anyway, but I never go past joking.

They might put their hands on me, but I never put my hands on one of them. I know they mean it, too. I went home with this woman once. I was mad at my old lady about some foolishness. I don't even remember what it was, but I was mad at her and there's this white lady at work who had been after me and after me for almost a year.

She was nice-looking, too. Her boss knew she was after me, but there wasn't anything he could do about it. They can't fire me. They could fire me but they wouldn't fire me. So I went over to her house and I drank and drank, and I was going to go ahead and do it when I got drunk enough, but I kept talking about my wife and talking about my wife until she finally gave me my coat and told me she thought I should go on home.

After that, she told me if I ever ran into another man like me to send him her way. She didn't care if he was black or white. She would marry him. She was a lot of fun, but I think the reason they fired her is because she would always be messing around with me. I don't know where that woman went. She was a nice lady.

I don't think I could ever marry a white lady, though. I'm prejudiced in a way, but then in a way I'm not. I got both races under me and I'll crack the whip on a black boy just as quick as I would a white boy.

Sure, I get bored. Variety is the spice of life. You come home tired and sometime you get tired of looking at the same woman but—you probably won't believe this either—but I make love to my wife almost every night, for ten years. She's just a sweet woman to make love to.

What bugs me sometime is that after ten years she still won't make the first move in love-making. She waits for me. She has never made the first move in all that time. Not once that I can remember.

She's always ready, though. I have a beer to slow me down, because she take a long time to get her nut. I drink beer and kiss her and we roll on into it.

She gets on top sometimes, but not much. We try fancy stuff sometimes, but neither one of us like it better than plain, ordinary lovin'.

She's colder than I am, but I mess around until she gets warm. I learned how to wait for her. You know who told me how? The preacher in Kentucky.

That's another reason I know she loves me. When we first got married I didn't have the experience to wait. I was ashamed sometimes, because I knew she wasn't getting satisfaction, but she never said anything about it to me.

It was just one time when in talking to the preacher about some problems I was having on base with my commanding officer, who didn't like niggers. He was from Moultrie, Georgia. Hated niggers and had an outfit that was over half black.

I was in talking to the preacher, and he just started talking about marriage and the nature of women. He put it all in a biblical context, talking about Abraham and Sarah and Hagar, but he got the message across about the nature of a woman.

Louisville, Kentucky, and her boss when she used to work out at the signal depot. She's not the kind to give up pussy that easy.

It took me two years to get it. Two years of steady work. I would leave her house sometimes so frustrated I wanted to knock down telephone poles with my fist. We'd just be kissing and kissing until we were hotter than firecrackers, but she would keep those legs crossed.

I know I musta almost broken her knees sometimes trying to uncross her legs. I'd have my johnson out in my hand, but she kept it locked up tight. Then, one time, in the back seat of her mother's car, she got weak. We were down in the woods near Magothy church. They were having camp meeting.

People had come from all over: Maryland, Virginia, Eastern Shore. I used to drive her mother's car, taking her grandfather back and forth to church. They would stay in church almost all night and we would sleep in the car until the old people got out, and we would run all over the campground. Women would be selling homemade food, anything you want: chicken, ham, sweet-potato pie, potato salad.

The Indians would have a tent selling herbs, and root doctors would be out there. Buses from all over would be there, and the kids would be fucking each other in back of the buses while the other kids were keeping watch to make sure they didn't get caught.

But camp meetings were fun. We used to have them every summer. Each week, they would be at a different church, out in the country. This was better than a country fair, because you could stay all night. When I got in my late teen-age years I didn't go as much. I used to play softball on the weekends. That was one thing.

But I remember this night, my wife's mother said I could use her car if I carried her father to camp meeting and picked him up when it was time to come home. My wife was with me when we dropped her grandfather off. She wasn't my wife then. We drove a little ways away, down by the missile site, because at that time they had all these missile sites back in the woods. They once had missiles in them that were sup-

Now it's nice. He said you have to stay with a woman, or some crap like that, or hang with a woman, or he told the story about Jacob, or somebody, wrestling with the angel, and Jacob told the angel, "I will not let you go until you bless me." The preacher went round about, but when I got home I wrestled with the angel and I didn't let her go, pregnant and all. And she blessed me. I stroked the bush with the rod until it caught on fire. That was the greatest feeling of my life. My wife was so happy that she cried and cried. She told me that she was never going to leave me. I became a husband that night. That's what husband means. You look it up in the dictionary. It means to plow, plant, to tend and make grow, bloom. Where do you think the word husbandry comes from?

I mean, we been through things. And then I got out of the service and we lived with her folks for more than a year, until we saved enough money to buy the house where we live now. You know who saved the money? My wife did. She don't waste shit. She'll tell you in a minute, "My old man works too hard for his money to be throwing it away like that." But the truth is, I don't work that hard. I appreciate her saying it, but I have a soft job in many ways.

I work around the house and I like to work on cars, that's what I do for recreation. I believe in God and I think marriage is sacred and sex is sacred. I don't go out and do something just because everyone else is doing it.

I only went with one woman before I got married—that's really in a full sexual way. You know how you lie when you're a teen-ager and say that you went with this girl and that girl. I used to lie like that, but I've only been with one woman sexually other than my wife.

This was a girl who lived not far from where my wife lived. She was younger than my wife but faster. I went with her when I was about seventeen and she was about eleven. That's the truth. She was only eleven years old, but she was built like a grown woman. I know this woman right now. She tried to get me to go with her when I first came out of the service, but I didn't.

My wife has never been with another man. I know that for a fact, though many have tried. Including the preacher in

A Love Affair   13

posed to shoot down any enemy planes that tried to bomb Washington or the Sparrow's Point steel factory. But, just before that, they had taken all of the missiles out and taken down the barbed-wire fences. They had signs up warning you not to trespass on government property, but we didn't pay any attention to those, because there weren't any missiles.

We went down in the dirt road and I begged her to let me have some and she said if I promised to marry her if she got pregnant. And I said I wanted to marry her even if she didn't get pregnant. So that was the first time. I got her cherry. I still got teeth marks on the side of my hand where she almost bit the meat off the side of my hand.

Now that I think back on it, we should have waited. She still feels guilty about that. We never talk about it. I mean, we go on as if our honeymoon, at the Howard Johnson's Motel, was our first time, but it wasn't.

We got married and checked into the motel. That was the first year that they would let black people stay in white motels in Maryland. We thought that was a big deal. At that time it was. We got the bridal suite. I carried her across the threshold, the whole thing.

She's a good woman. What else can I say? She's like her mother in that respect. You can tell a lot about the way a woman will treat you if you watch the way her mother treats her father. My daddy taught me that. "See how her mother treats her father and that's how she'll treat her man."

Maria's mother and father are still in love for that matter. They've been married forty years. They still have sex two or three times a week. I know, because when we were living there they would turn the radio on every time they were going to have sex, to drown out the noise.

They get it on. I only hope that Maria and I will be doing half as good when we get in our sixties.

2

By Any Other Name

Something grew, even in that deep shade.

"If you want to talk about hate," Valery Adams said in the measured, precise way she had of saying things. "If you want to talk about hate. I could talk for hours about a man I absolutely hate. Anything can be defined in terms of its opposite, so I could define love by telling you about this man.

"You know how when you love someone you can close your eyes and picture their face. Well, I can close my eyes and picture the face of this Negro. I hate him and I know exactly why I hate him," she said.

She has a plump, wide face and dimples. She is yellowish brown with freckles. Her dress was carelessly ironed, carelessly fitted, carelessly chosen in the first place, since its odd, greenish color would look better on a darker person.

She is talkative. She has attempted suicide twice in the past three years, indicating that her $18,000-per-year middle-management job, her expensive apartment, and her $2,000 concert upright piano have been poor hedges against depression.

She got up from the sofa. The ridges around the sofa's cushions had made jagged red lines along the backs of her thighs. She went to the kitchen to make more coffee. A Stevie Wonder album was playing in the apartment down the hall.

I came to the kitchen door to watch her. She measured the right amount of coffee for the percolator. She is a very precise person in some ways but in others, in matters of appearance or neatness she doesn't seem to care a great deal. Her apartment is a mess.

"I can tell you why I hate him," her voice flew upward to say.

"Why?" I asked, still leaning against the doorjamb.

"Let me start from the beginning. It was two years ago in the winter. It was a time in my life when I absolutely didn't know if I wanted to live or die. This man, this parasite used every skill at his command to manipulate my helplessness simply because he wanted to fuck me," she said. "Plain and simple."

It seemed that she hadn't been saying words like fuck for long. The word sounded new in her mouth like motherfucker in the mouth of an Englishman.

The opposite wall of her large living room was covered with books. I went over and looked at some of the titles. Many of the books were general books about the psychology of living, written from various points of view, discussing various aspects, implying various solutions to the problems of the intelligent urban human being. Outside, the rain was still falling on the freeway that ran next to the service road that bordered the building.

"That's what sent me off to the psychiatrist in the first place," she said. "I found myself waking up in the morning in my bed, in my apartment, looking at this man." She threw her hands in the air. The rise and fall of her voice made her conversation like a public recital. She was standing in the kitchen doorway. The big, lazy cat asleep on the piano must have been used to her voice. He did not even open an eye to acknowledge her ranting.

"And I knew I didn't love him. I never did love him. I met him in the winter of 1970. I had just come to the city from Southern California. I remember because it was snowing and I hadn't been close to snow for two years. It was snowing like crazy. I remember it coming in from the airport. You know how it snows in New York: dirty snow. Dirty even before it hits the ground." She laughed at this observation. She laughed almost hysterically, with the rain coming down and gleaming in the headlights of the cars moving rapidly along the freeway. She came back to the sofa with two cups of coffee. I tasted mine. It was good even without cream. I added cream and sugar as I listened to her.

"Anyway, I got a place at the YWCA, the one on East Forty-fifth Street near where all the prostitutes hang out along in front of the Press Box Restaurant. I could see those chicks from my window. Some of them were nice-looking, too, out there in the cold with the big coats and the little miniskirts.

"They would scatter like birds when the police came down the street, and slowly gather again once the police were gone, all in a row waiting for men to come by and get them. I used to watch all this in my room from my window. It was funny, and at the same time it was sad. That's what I did every night until I fell asleep.

"I didn't know why I had come to New York. Actually, I hated New York. I've always hated the city. Maybe that's why I came. I was determined to stay here to prove something, I guess."

"During the day, I hit the streets looking for an apartment and at night I just laid up in my room watching the whores. I found this apartment in about a week. I liked it because it was away from everything. Maybe I was subconsciously preparing to commit suicide then. Maybe that's why I took an apartment way out here."

"Way out here in the rain," I said.

"And snow. You remember it snowed a lot during the winter of 1970. At that time I didn't know anyone in New York. My father lived out in Long Island, but I know I didn't come to the city to be close to him. He didn't even know I was in New York—nobody did. My mother was in Georgia. She thought I was still in California." The rising and falling of Valery's voice gave a strange rhythm to her words. She was a strange lady. Fiercely intelligent, friendly but not quite sociable, as if she had been off somewhere and had not been talking to people lately.

Too much privacy surrounded her and her cat. I'm sure that she didn't have many friends among her neighbors, who were mostly older, middle-class Jews.

"After I got set up in this apartment, I didn't have this much furniture, but my books were on their way from California, so I guess that means that subconsciously I was planning to make the move to New York more or less permanent. I got the place set up well enough to live in, and then I decided to go to this party in the Bronx given by this white girl from where I worked, at McCullum's.

"It was a weird party. Most of the people were young white kids. There were a few older people there, but mostly young people. It was nice. I was glad I came. I needed to be around people. There were two or three West Indian guys, but mostly college-age hippies jumping around. I think the girl who gave the party was living with a West Indian guy. All of the food was West Indian: Jamaican peas and rice, curried goat.

"But there was this one older black man. He was in the dining room talking to two white girls with weird makeup and long black dresses and a lot of beads and shit, dressed like two witches, and I learned later that they like to fuck the same man at the same time. This black guy they were talking to kept looking at me while he was talking to them, looking over their shoulders at me. I wish now they had ended up with him that night." She laughed.

"But that night I was very lonely. I had my new furniture, so I could have company for the first time. I was tired of being alone. He was a handsome man, intelligent-looking, tall, slender, with a graying Afro." She mocked him. "Distinguished. Maybe because he was older, maybe because he was black and I had just begun thinking racially after trying for four years to stop thinking racially. Anyway, I let him know that I was digging him too," she said.

The buzzer to the door downstairs rang. She spoke on the intercom. It was her present boy friend. He was on his way up. "Hey," she said, "put the tape recorder away. I don't want Eric to think I was telling you things about him. Not until I clear it with him. I'm sure he wouldn't mind, but I'd rather ask him first," she said.

"Sure, but he's not the same guy you hate?"

"No . . . no, not him." She laughed. Her personality seemed to have changed completely. There was something childish about her as she waited for her boy friend to come up.

"So what's the worry? You weren't talking about him."

"But I'm planning to. I'll ask him if it's all right. She got up and unlocked the door. "I'll call you when I can talk again," she said. "I enjoyed the talk but there's more to it." Her boy friend, a small dark-skinned man, came through the unlocked door.

I chatted for a while with the two of them. He said that he thought love to be the strongest force on earth. "But you're freaky anyway, Eric," she said and giggled playfully. He said he wouldn't mind being interviewed. He wished me luck with the book. I left and drove back to Manhattan.

For the rest of the evening, I wandered around the Village looking up at lighted windows, wondering how many people had solved the problem, at least temporarily, and how many had simply locked themselves in with nothing but a dog or a cat for company, having decided that people are more trouble than their company is worth.

Historians say that a decline in a civilization is usually marked by an increase in the number of pets. In the Village it was almost impossible to walk without stepping in or around a pile of dog shit. I remember how the hippies used to plant little American flags in those piles, as if they were captured hills on a battlefield.

There were sections of the upper East Side that were worse than the Village. Most of the people who lived in these sections were white. It had always seemed that whites were fifty years ahead of us in adapting to loneliness, but we were gaining. More and more, you could see manicured black men out walking their manicured dogs. The men walked as if they had blinders, as if they no longer cared to search the faces of passers-by. Only the dogs were looking for companionship with their own kind or a friendly fire hydrant to wet against.

It was late when I got to the small, empty apartment on Ninth Street that I had rented. The drapery was drawn back, exposing the burglary bar across the windows. It was a small place that had originally been a hallway. Now it doubled as a $200-per-month efficiency apartment and a main highway for roaches moving from the air shaft in the back to the kitchen of the apartment in front.

The place seemed to give perfect dimensions to the isolation I felt. I had been talking to too many lonely or cynical people in the past two weeks. It was like that. There would be weeks when I'd run into a string of people who thought that love was wonderful, and weeks when everyone seemed to be playing games, and then weeks like the past two, when I'd get the impression that people would be better off if they forgot about love and found some other way to relate to each other.

I was in the apartment a few days later transcribing tapes when the phone rang. "Hey, have you got some time tonight?" Valery Adams asked. "We could finish the interview. I think it's fun. I talked with my friend about the book. He said I should send you around to see his wife. She would have some jokes for your book." Valery giggled.

That night at nine o'clock I went back to see her. I played the tail end of the other tape so she could take up where we left off. "Oh! The party, yeah, that's where I met the creep."

"The one you hate more than you love anyone on earth."

"I didn't say that. I love my friend Eric, the one you met—but I can't get this other Negro out of my mind. When you asked me about love I instantly thought about him. I think I'm a negative person. Anyway I think of negative things before I think of positives ones. . . ."

"How was the party?" I asked.

"It was a nice party. All these young white girls were dressed in costumes and shit, and everyone was smoking pot and inhaling helium to make their highs nicer. They say that'll give you a better high. That was the first time I'd ever seen that. People were dancing wild and smoking pot. There was more pot there than I had seen in a long time, and they were inhaling helium from balloons. When the balloons were empty, they'd run back to the kitchen and get them refilled from a tank and run back to the dance floor. It was really a loud, wild scene.

"For sure, the party made me stop feeling sorry for myself. Streamers were hanging from the ceiling, acid rock was blaring from the stereo, people coming in and out. The kitchen was full of spicy West Indian food: curried goat, pickled souse, breadfruit—everything. And rum punch. Lots of rum punch. People were eating food with their hands.

"I was getting a contact high just from being around all that pot and food and noise, and this dude was just digging me, watching every move I made even though he was still talking to the witching twins. I was rapping, dancing, getting into it and digging him digging me. He was standing near the kitchen door, and one time when I was on my way to the kitchen he caught my arm and ask me to fix him a plate of food. I told him sure I'd do it. I piled the stuff on his plate—a little bit of everything.

"Then I came back and did this really seductive dance right

in front of him. He introduced me to the witching twins. Their names were Tanya and Tonya, so they said. When I got up close I could see that they probably weren't even sisters, much less twins, but they were dressed alike.

"After the party, he came home with me and we talked all night into the morning. That was my mistake. I should've let him fuck me and sent him on his way," she laughed.

"But instead you fell in love with him."

"No, no. I never did love him. That's the thing. He was either very clever or I was more desperate than I thought, but in about three days he had the keys to my apartment and I would come home from work and there would be this Negro laying in my bed sleeping like a baby." This time she laughed at *herself*.

"What I don't know is how I used to come home and cook supper for him. I used to think about him at work. I don't know what happened. I wasn't in love with him, but I used to think about him all the time."

"Maybe it was sexual?" I said. "Maybe that's why you didn't put him out. Did you try to put him out?"

"That's not easy when you're lonely," she argued in a voice that made her statement almost a question or a plea. "A lot of men blackmail women like that. The usual way, however, is when the guy is sexually incompetent and he'll blackmail you into saying that he's not. 'Do you like this? Do you like that?' One of these times I'm tempted to say: 'No, get up.'" She laughed. Part of her hysteria returned with her laughter.

"You think you could do that?" I asked, thinking that it would be a good thing to do. I could imagine how surprised the man would be. I laughed.

"No, unfortunately. I could never do that"; she sat up straight on the sofa. "And anyway he was very, very good. He was the kind of person who would delay his climax to make sure you got two or three before he got one. He was the kind of man who would go without pleasure in order to give pleasure."

"What's wrong with that?"

"Nothing, except that most people like that give pleasure in order to get power. They don't want pleasure. They'd rather let you enjoy yourself so they can have power over you. It's a form of sexual fascism."

"Okay, I know what you mean," I said. I had interviewed a man who told me he had fallen in love with a woman like that. She gave pleasure in order to get power, which in turn gave her security and freedom—the security that the man would never leave her because she worked so hard at pleasing him, and the freedom to leave him because she never allowed him to please her. I told Valery about this. She said that's precisely what she meant.

"Then, why didn't you insist that he allow you to please him, too," I asked.

"Unfortunately, I'm not the kind of person who insists on anything. I can never do that, just as I can never stop him from calling here."

"I didn't know you still talked to him."

"He still calls every once in a while."

"Why don't you tell the police to make him stop calling?"

"That's what I just said," she said desperately. "I'm not the type person who can do that, and he knows this, and he knows if he ever got inside my apartment, I'm not the kind of person who could force him to leave, so he keeps calling, and I know why he calls. He calls hoping one day he'll find that same little jelly fragment of a person that he can manipulate into going to bed with him. Aw-w-w-w, I hate him.

"You should interview him. That's what you should do. He would love that. I know what he would say. He would be very smug about himself. He would tell you that he'd rather give than receive. He'd tell you how unselfish he is and all the elaborate reasons why he's so unselfish and hopelessly self-sacrificing."

"What if I'd ask him about you?"

"He would say he sat with me during a very difficult period in my life, a very suicidal period, and how he still loves me and calls every so often to make sure I'm all right. So, apparently, he's too dense to know that I hate his guts." She paused for a moment, thought for a moment. She looked strangely younger than she was. The plump brown cheeks looked almost like baby fat. In the dim lamplight her freckles were barely visible. The freckles did, I remember, add a pleasant element to her face, mostly because she seemed a little too dark to be having freckles in the first place.

Her eyes seemed a little red from cigarette smoke, but she was not still smoking. The ash tray on the coffee table was full, but not one of the cigarettes in it had been smoked down to the butt. Each had been snuffed out about midway, bent violently back so that brown crimps of tobacco bulged out of the torn skin. I asked her if she had been awake all last night.

She said she had. "But no one man was responsible for my nervous breakdown," she said. "I'm not going to blame it all on this man. I wouldn't want to give him that much credit. He simply took advantage of my weakened state while I was on my way to having it. Actually, my childhood set me up for a nervous breakdown. The actual process started when I went to California, at sixteen. This white man, my freshman literature professor, Roger Guillaume—he started the process as far as men are concerned. He was the first man I ever said 'I love you' to. That includes my father. Roger was the first man I ever said 'I love you' to and really meant it.

"In high school I was very good. I got very good grades. I went to a private boarding school in North Carolina for colored girls." She said "colored" as if it tasted like acid in her mouth. We were now sitting on her sofa. She was ready to talk for a long time. Potato chips had been placed on the table, and beside the wooden potato-chip bowl was a Mason jar full of marijuana mixed with little bits of hashish.

She said, "I *pay* my psychiatrist for listening to this same shit. I might as well let you listen for free. It's odd that even though I was reared in the South I was very, very protected. I had a sheltered childhood. We lived in one of those big, southern middle-class homes in Atlanta where the 'right' music is listened to, the 'right' books are present but never read, and 'good' English is spoken.

"It was a very protected life. The women almost never went downtown. They were seldom confronted with the realities of racism, you see. All the shopping was done in the 'colored' neighborhood, all the socializing was in the homes of the people my mother's family had known for years. It's a closed world.

"Then men left home each morning in suit and tie to go downtown to their menial jobs. They suffered the indignities, or they did their little 'Uncle Tom' number, but they never brought that home. In the neighborhood they were Mr. C. W. Brown, or Deacon L. A. Anderson, or some phony shit like that. It was all so unreal. The women were protected until they were above the age of sexual interest, and then if the family needed money, they were sent off to work in the kitchen of some 'quality' white people, or to be the nanny of some white brats.

"If the family had some money, the women never came in contact with the real world. I was raised by women who seldom came in contact with the real world. I was born in the North, in Freeport, Long Island, but when my father and mother separated I was taken to Georgia to live with my mother's folks. For the nine years I was in Long Island, I was suffering under the illusion that I was free. Then, when I got to Georgia, I found out there were a lot of things I couldn't do because I was black. I was furious. From the time I got there I was furious. I guess it was then that I got the idea that by marrying a white man I would escape some of this.

"These were the conditions under which I met Roger. I was living in sunny Santa Barbara, one of the most racist sections of California. I was living in this big old house with two white roommates. I was planning to major in English literature, and Roger, even though he was French, was my freshman English professor.

"I liked being out there. I liked being free for the first time since I was nine. We had a nice house with palm trees in the front yard and fruit trees in the back. I was in heaven. Sixteen years old. Dumb as a chicken, in heavenly California.

"I was fascinated by Roger from the first day. You can imagine. He was young, delicate, and very intellectual. The exact opposite to what I had been used to, and he was white.

"But at the same time I was fascinated by this black guy named G. Willard Grant. He was so cool, man. Everything I'd been raised to adore, with the pipe and the tweed jacket, even in the California heat. He had the little sports car. He was tall. He was neat. He was really black. He spoke 'good' English and he listened to good jazz.

"The only problem was that I was awed by him. I was frightened to death. He was twenty-four years old, and I knew he was just playing with me. Such a God-awful bastard he was! Every time I tried to talk to him I could feel that he was laughing at me. I would say something like 'D. H. Lawrence should have included Mark Twain in his *Studies in Classic American Literature*. I would love to see him deal with Huck Finn and Nigger Jim.'

"G. Willard Grant would sit and look at me and smile condescendingly. He wouldn't say anything, and even today I wonder, do men like him not say anything because they're cool or because they don't know what to say? I suspect the latter. Being cool is a way of hiding your ignorance. The thing is, though, they can make you feel like a fool fluttering around in front of them with these little ideas that they can make seem so unimportant.

"He said he was from New York, but now I suspect he was from Mississippi," she laughed. "I don't know why he kept coming to the house anyway, unless it was to screw one of my white roommates. I never really went out with him, but I adored him. He used to come over and sit and watch the stupidest programs on television and laugh at the dumbest things. He could sit for hours grinning at 'The Dick Van Show.'" She laughed again.

"I never did go to bed with him. I was afraid to. I knew that this man—so tall, so black, so handsome—could probably be very cruel if you'd let yourself fall in love with him. My father was like that—a very handsome man. He was tall and light-skinned, but he reminded me somewhat of G. Willard Grant. He could be as selfish and cold as ice.

"But to really understand my fears you have to go back to D. H. Lawrence's theory of blood-memory. A woman's blood remembers or gets used to one man, and then the woman doesn't want any other man to touch her. It's true. Every woman has periods in her life when she wants to take a man into her blood, and the man that she allows in at that time gets everything—gets it all. It doesn't matter if he's bad for her; he gets everything. If necessary, she'll impute qualities to him that he doesn't really have just to justify her addiction to him.

"That's why women have to be careful about who they let in. That's why many women are frightened of a man they can't control. Because once he's in there he can drive her to suicide. He can misuse her for years, with her friends telling her that the man's no damn good.

"That's why many very handsome men, like G. Willard Grant, are frightened and have such a hard time getting women, whereas an unspectacular person like Roger seems safe enough. I felt eminently acceptable to Roger, and as a person I thought I could control him. At least he was not cruel. I could easily have been as cruel as he was.

"And he was a very involved person, whereas G. Willard Grant was only involved with himself. I was flattered by Roger's attention to me. We would stay after class discussing D. H. Lawrence or Coleridge, and this is what I loved to do at the time.

"Then, before long, he was inviting me to his apartment to talk about literature. He lived just as I'd always thought a professor would live: in a little apartment not far from the campus, by himself, with every room in the house crammed full of books. Every time we talked about something he would pull a book down from the wall and quote something that Blake or Browning or Byron had said on that particular subject. I idolized him.

"He looked like my ideal of a professor, with the tennis shoes, jeans, and red hair, and the little red beard. He hated faculty meetings. He was more concerned about his students than he was about tenure and academic policy. He was a campus rebel, in other words.

"Then it was one night when I was over there. He had built

a fire in his little hibachi and we were toasting hot dogs and talking when he decided to do something he had obviously been planning to do for a long time. That was when I lost my virginity, at seventeen, in his apartment, with Camus, Sartre, and Blake looking down from the bookshelves." She laughed. "I hope they enjoyed what they saw. This was the only time I went to bed with Roger. Two months later, I found out I was pregnant." She paused for a while remembering this, or remembering something that she was not going to tell me.

"So there I was an almost-virgin who has to go and get an abortion because this man had lied to me. He had told me we were going to be married, and I believed him. Then, after I got pregnant, I found out that he was a homosexual, and I was the third woman he had been with in his life. What a mess!

"In his defense, if I care to defend him, if I remember him well enough to want to defend him, he had no idea that I was a virgin. There was no blood on the sheets. I wasn't afraid. I was in love. I was seventeen and about to be married to a very mature man. He was a Catholic and didn't believe in birth control, and I was a great D. H. Lawrence naturalist who didn't want anything artificial, like a condom, between me and the man I loved.

"So, a couple of weeks after that, G. Willard Grant drove me down to Los Angeles in his Austin-Healey and I got an abortion from a midwife. This was my terrible introduction to love.

"If I ever was going to become a Lesbian, that would have been the time. I hated men.

"One of the girls and I used to sit up talking about men. We were both very confused, and I think we did love each other. We talked about sleeping together. I think she really loved me. I used to dream about her and that frightened me, and in the end we were both too young and frightened to do anything.

"It was about a year from then before I had anything to do with men. I came to Long Island during the summer of 1967 to stay with my father. He was the one who convinced me that I had to get myself together. I hadn't planned to tell him what happened, but during the course of things I did tell him. I remember it was on his fishing boat, off Montauk. I told him the whole mess; then I broke down and cried in the arms of this man who I'd seen only about three times in my life since I was nine years old.

"He's a very handsome man. An Adam Clayton Powell-type Negro. I love him. I don't know why I should, but I love him. He gave some of the best advice that anyone could have given. He told me that I should go out and find myself a man. He said it rather bluntly. He said, 'You'd better let someone make love to you, Janet'—that's my middle name. He likes it better than Valery. I do, too.

"'Just go out and find a man that you can care something about and go to bed with him,' he said. 'You're young. You can't let this one thing ruin your life.' That was cold, coming from your own father, but it was good advice.

"About a week later, I found this pretty little black lieutenant at the Air Force base. I went to his BOQ room and gave him everything. I didn't enjoy it. I'm sure he didn't. I took the pill, used vaginal jelly, foam, and made him use a rubber to make sure I wouldn't get pregnant again." She laughed.

"On top of that, I was stiff as a board, petrified, afraid that despite the jelly, the foam, and the rubber something would happen. I was twenty years old. Life is funny. I was twenty and had had only two sexual experiences in my life, but somehow I felt that there was nothing more I wanted out of love.

"I became a missionary. With the other men I met I became a missionary. I got in a habit of going out with weak men, men who I felt needed *me*. I would sleep with a man if he wanted me to, for whatever the reason. I became a mother, a fucking mother." She laughed, mocking herself.

"Now that I think of it, that must have been part of what bruised me, letting all those men get off on me without ever thinking about what I needed, what I wanted. I guess there were about twelve of them, looking for a mother. I even dreamed of finding Roger and reforming his homosexuality. I started going to church again—as my grandmother used to say, 'Jesus is first, others are second, and I am third.' I put myself dead last in every relationship.

"It was both white and black guys. I was trying not to think racially then, or rather, one month I was fiercely black and I'd join the Black Arts Theatre on campus, and the next month I would be a universalist, back dating white boys again. That's why I say I might be too selfish to really love anyone right now—if you mean by love something self-sacrificing, some bullshit about giving your all to someone," she laughed. "I don't think I'm ever going to do that, ever again."

She got up and went to the kitchen to fix tea. "Despite all this I still think of myself as a loving person," she said. She came to the kitchen door. "I just don't call it love. I don't even like to talk about love." She laughed. "You noticed that, huh?" My family loved me: they loved me so much that I couldn't play with certain kids; they loved me so much that I had to go to the best private schools; they loved me so much that I had to get straight A's," she said, and pulled her head back into the kitchen again.

I rolled two jays while she was gone. "They loved me so much that my mother, in her old age, worked her fingers to the bone to give me the best, as she is constantly reminding me." She came back and put the cups of tea on the table. "So, no. Don't talk to me about love," she said as she sat down. "I don't like to use the word. I'm not even looking for a substitute for it. All I deal with now are relationships—and they are either good ones or bad ones, depending on how they make me feel," she said.

I lighted one of the jays and filled my mouth and lungs with smoke. "What kind of relationship makes you feel good?" I asked without exhaling. I handed her the reefer. She took a drag and held it in her mouth as she spoke. "Ones where there is no commitment of any kind. No obligations. You come together because you want to be together. There's no money changing hands. No vows being taken. My man now, Eric, the guy you saw the first time you were here. He and I have a relationship like that. I don't call it love, because I can go for weeks without seeing the man, and I don't even think about him for weeks at a time, and you're *not* supposed to be able to do *that* if you're in love.

"I enjoy not having to adjust to another person's going and coming, not having to fix my hair or my head because James is coming over, not having to worry about whether or not the way I am is affecting the way Arnold is, whether I am injuring John or putting him down or making him feel inadequate or castrated because I am so intelligent.

"I've known Eric for two years. I met him in the elevator of this building about a year ago. He was looking pretty good, so I struck up a conversation. I'd finally gotten rid of the creep who'd moved in on me—the creep who sent me to the psychiatrist. No, let me put it this way: I had gotten the creep out of my apartment because the psychiatrist told me if I didn't, he was going to drive me to suicide again."

"You committed suicide once?" I laughed.

She laughed. "I tried." She held out her hands. There were two small scars on her wrist. "Anyway, I had gotten this creep out of my apartment, but he was still calling. It was like having a buzzard circling over you on the desert." She laughed again as smoke from the reefer curled up toward her eyes. "So Eric came home with me the first time so he could curse the creep out when he called.

"After that, we started a nice little friendship. I knew in the long run that he was no good for me. He was married and going to stay married. He was weird. In many ways he didn't speak to parts of my personality that I wanted to bring into a relationship.

"He was such a mysterious little man. He's thirty-five and married to a West Indian chick. The side of him that she's developed is the side I can't use. What I like about him is that he's perfectly relaxed. If he comes here and I'm not in a mood to talk, he'll sit and read and then leave, or he might bring a record over and play it until I get in another mood, if I'm ever going to that night.

"He keeps some of the best smoke in the world right here in Mama's jar. But, like I said, I resisted him for a long time. I blocked him out. I presented him with only a certain segment of me. For one thing, I wouldn't let myself climax when I was with him. I didn't want to get him into my blood. I was doing my angel-of-mercy number, giving without even wanting to enjoy it myself. The horrible paradox is that he overrode that. He didn't override it in any forceful, breaking way. He overrode it by ignoring it, and by being exquisitely competent, and terribly self-assured." She laughed at herself being very analytic.

"He's not a handsome man, but he's cute in a rugged, hairy sort of little way. I like his eyes. He has very nice, almost oriental eyes, and I discovered that I liked not having to worry about *his* ego in a sexual relationship, not having to give him signs and signals that he is a good lover.

"I liked not having to give flattery. So I gradually learned to like him. Then I began to notice little things about him, like after we've made love and we shift positions and his penis is soft, he'd put it against me, which most men would never do. Most men immediately hide or want to hide their penis when it is not erect," she laughed. "They get back in the shorts or back under the sheets. Even men with very large penises hide shamefully like little boys when the penis is not erect.

"Oh, when it's erect they like to strut around the room with it. They want everyone to see them in their mighty power. It's something I've watched over the years and found to be really fascinating. But Eric was the first man I met who was self-confident enough to make love with a soft penis, without panic, which was a wonderfully relaxing sensation. He said, 'Don't worry, it'll be ready when it wants to be.'

"I told this story to several women, experienced women, one of them had been married for eight years and her husband had never done it. Their reaction was the same as mine: 'Goddamn, finally, a together man!'" She smiled disarmingly, like a little girl.

"Then, you *are* in love."

She looked at me for a moment, exasperated. "What did I just get finished telling you? No!"

"I've got this fabulous devil flying in for the weekend from Nashville, Tennessee," he says and sucks his teeth. Devil is his term of endearment for a white woman. "So you know I'll be on the slopes until Monday morning." On the slopes means skiing, which means that he'll be making love to a snow, a "snow" being his other term of endearment for a white woman.

"Then, next weekend, I have to catch the Eastern Airline shuttle to New York"—he narrows his eyes to let his listener savor the significance of New York, the premier city of the world—"to meet this fabulous coal. Lives on West Seventy-eighth Street near the Museum of Natural History." He laughs and sucks his teeth again. Coal is his term of endearment for a black woman.

He is a player who shuttles back and forth among a constantly changing number of snows and coals and Buddha-heads. He is a jet-setter, not of the 747 international jumbo jets, but of the smaller DC-9's that shuttle back and forth between Washington, where he lives and plays, and New York and Boston, where he also plays.

He is a jet-setter who never leaves the United States. He's afraid to leave, because he's a West Indian with possible visa problems, and he doesn't like to take the risk that he might not be allowed back into the United States, to the smör-gåsbord he loves.

"Then, on Wednesday night, I've got to meet the wife of the cultural attaché of ——————." He paused to let the impact of that vibrate in the air. "She wants to see me while her husband is away shuttling back and forth between Budapest and Istanbul. While he's shuttling she wants to experience the big bamboo." The big bamboo is his term of endearment for his penis. "Thirty-two-year-old French chick. She's not wealthy, but she has the social connections which can be translated into money." His voice has a West Indian lilt.

"I've only stroked her once—from midnight to four in the morning. When we finished she took the bamboo in her hand

and said, '*Magnifique, magnifique,*'" he laughs. "The big bamboo-oo-oo," he says.

He is not handsome. His attraction is that he is very tall and now, at home, naked to the waist, serenely black, muscular, unusual. There's no doubt that women in airports turn to look at him. He is then dressed too well to be a highjacker, yet he looks a little too unconventional to be a businessman.

His reddish leather boots add two inches to his height. People turn to look a second time to see if they really see what they think they saw. Yes, he *is* that tall. He smiles down at them. He is six foot five, but with the boots and his Afro he looks six eight.

And he *is* that black—almost as black as coal—and smooth-skinned and pampered, with a great deal of dignity to his walk when he's not bopping along letting his midi-length gray suede coat swing along behind him.

He is unusual enough to make them wonder. Some don't want to let him see them looking, but he whirls around suddenly and catches them anyway before they can drop their eyes back to their magazine. Reddish boots, gray coat, high Afro laughs when he catches them—the secretaries, nurses, college girls, and wives of cultural attachés.

"That's what she asked me," he says, sitting now on his beanbag chair. "I answered, 'I'm not tall, I'm long.'" He laughs. He likes the significance of that, because he likes to give the impression that he lives by his dick.

"I got lots of bitches, lots of bitches, and I love each one of them, in my way," he warns. "Love for me is a very warm feeling, a feeling of concern that you have for someone. I have had that feeling many times. I've had that feeling six times *this* week. Every day. Twice on Tuesday, because I had two dates on Tuesday. O-o-o-o-ow," he laughs.

"You asked me about love, right? My feelings on love are just as valid as anyone else's. They're just as valid as those people who say that love has to be something permanent. Who says that marriage is the pinnacle of love? Love and marriage are two separate things. Marriage is a legal agreement between two legal adults. It has nothing to do with love. In fact, it is the fastest way to kill love.

"I love each bitch I—You take a man who screwed his wife six times this week. Did he feel more love than I did for the six women I screwed this week? Six bitches, man. Six. No. I showed more concern. I gave more pleasure. I fucked them better. If he's been married for longer than a short while, he probably takes his wife for granted. He's down there to satisfy himself. I never take a woman for granted. Never. Never. Never." He laughs.

He is a divided man, perhaps, a fragmented man with no neat lines to mark off his self-divisions. A large sliver of him is, no doubt, a comical braggart, the kind who wants to make you feel that encounters with the wives of cultural attachés occur as often as encounters with $9,000-per-year secretaries.

Yet a large part of him is serious, too, and stable beneath the shifting surface of the personality that flows outward onto the world. "No, I don't equate love and sex. They are quite distinct in my mind. I am not controlled by either love or sex. I control both of them, and sex is an extension of the love I feel for certain female persons." He laughs. He is proud of that definition.

"I always love, but I go in spurts with sex. I make love only when I want to, because fucking is not that important to me, but when I fuck I do it in a way that makes it important. Sometimes I go for weeks without making love. The pussy piles up, and then I have to have time to unstack it, o-o-o-o-ow."

Words zing from him. His tone is philosophical each time before he bursts into laughter. The serious side of him is very philosophical, and stable enough to have earned him a master's degree in economics. His hobby is raising house plants, watching their slow growth. He is very seldom absent from work, and very seldom late. He enjoys his job at a commercial-credit firm, where he does something as abstract and people-less as economic analysis of national trends and the effect of legislation on investment portfolios. But his leisure life is full of rushing people. He has two telephone lines coming into his Cleveland Park bachelor's apartment so he can put one woman on HOLD while he is talking to another.

"I love women. I love all types of women. Oh, man. Me? Yes. I was riding down Connecticut Avenue two days ago in a cab and I saw this ba-a-a-ad sister, strutting. She was strutting, man. I wanted to leap out of the cab and grab onto her and love her. The funny thing is I was already on my way to Georgetown to stroke this German monster on my lunch hour. Lounch hour." He pushes these words out until they become tangible but mashed and compressed by the urgency of his voice and the lilt of his accent.

"I love her too, oh, yeah. The gristle was as stiff as bamboo," he laughs.

"I'm a searcher and a seeker. I'm always searching and seeking for something different to bring into the rhythm of my life. The reason why it's so easy for me to move from one woman to another is that I don't keep changing my personality to fit each one of them. I make them change to fit me. I pull them into my rhythm, because if I changed to fit them, then I would be the weak one, wouldn't I? And I'm not weak. I'm strong; not cold but strong. If I were a cold person I would be emotionless, which is not true. I'm very, very emotional.

"I'm very emotional, and I don't think of myself as using women. I love them too much for that. I respect them too much for that. I give as much as I take. I give food. I give hospitality. I give them my time. I cook for them. Yes, soup. This soup is called conch soup. Curry mutton, cassava dumplings, mashed-potato pudding with the orange peel in it and the raisin. I give them my body. I'm in fine physical shape. I run ten miles a week. No fat. Ten miles man, ten miles. I smoke a little herb but I don't smoke cigarettes. I drink a little wine but no hard liquor. Maybe a little rum.

"I give to them yes, but I force them to give to me also; because they *must*. If I give to them while lusting after the sex, that would make me a trick. They must give me something. I don't ask them to *give* me gifts. I make them *bear* gifts.

Sometimes I meet them at the door and turn them around if they come bearing nothing.

"If they come bringing nothing, that means they've come to take and not give. Like the little devil from the Department of Health, Education and Welfare." He pushes the name out. He likes the accidental significance of her being from Health, Education and Welfare. He has the kind of abstract mind that finds accidental relationships between a lot of disparate things.

"I made her send to Holland to get a gold necklace for me. She came back from three weeks in Europe and brought me nothing, nothing but six silk handkerchiefs. I refused the handkerchiefs. She must get the necklace. She must get it or else. If she doesn't get it I'll repudiate her. I'll use that one little thing to put her in the doghouse. In the doghouse, man. How? I won't allow her to see me. I will deny her my beauty," he says and pauses to show that he is at least half serious, sitting there rocking in his beanbag chair, half naked.

"But there is this other woman who's coming down here tonight to bring a bottle of cologne. A fabulous sister from Housing and Urban Development," he laughs, because he likes the fact that she is from Housing and Urban Development. "HUD, fine bitch. I was with her last weekend. She stayed here. We loved for two nights and two days. I took care of her. Cooked. Conversated her.

"So she promised me this cologne. She actually went out and bought it, but then she said she's not going to give it to me because I didn't call her Monday or Tuesday or Wednesday. She said she had a beautiful weekend. I know she did. I made it beautiful, but then when I called her Thursday, she said—he imitates a woman's voice—'You didn't have to wait till Thursday to call.'" He laughs and puts on his thickest West Indian accent: "'If I don't call be cool. You have your life to live. Live that. Don't try to live mine.'

"So she is coming down tonight to bring the cologne, or she might not bring it. I don't know, but she won't get through the door without it. That's all I want from her: the cologne. What'll happen when she comes? Me, fuck her? No. I want the cologne. I'm dealing with the principle of it. I have enough money to buy cologne. In fact I have expensive oils and shit. But she promised me the cologne, or she goes in the doghouse. You got to keep them straight. You must make them give, because if they give then that leaves you free to give to them.

"When she came last weekend I had stocked the house with the best foods, I cooked for her. I bathed her. I don't care if it's a woman I see regularly, I train her to bring me little goodies every so often. That way I know she's thinking of me. If it's nothing more than a bottle of wine: 'Here, I bought you this.'

" 'For me?'

" 'Yes.' " He is play-acting.

" 'Good. Thank you. Let's have a little,' I say. That's a good opener. We can drink the wine. I can drink the wine while I'm in the kitchen cooking for her, or on the sofa looking at her telling her how beautiful she is, which is what she wants to hear, what all of them want to hear.

"You mustn't allow women to use that sex thing as payment for your being nice to them. You must remind them that most of the time a man, a good man, gives more than a woman in the sex act, anyway. She's not giving you anything. You're actually giving her something go-o-o-d, something that is quite scarce—some good gristle." He claps his hands and laughs. The beans crunch in his beanbag chair as it adjusts to his movement.

"So how can anyone say that I hate women? I love women, but I know them. I know women. How can you say I have a low opinion of women? I think like they do and I appreciate the way they scheme on men, but I don't let them scheme on me.

"No one you've interviewed loves women more than I do, man. Sometimes I'm sorry that I only have one dick. If I had three dicks I would station one of them in New York and one in Washington permanently, and then I would put one on temporary duty in Boston, California, and Chicago—o-o-o-ow.

"Sometimes I love women so much that I make three dates in one night. When I leave the house I haven't even decided which one I'm going to see that night. I might choose one of them for completely arbitrary reasons. I might choose this certain one because there is likely to be a parking spot in front of her house. I might choose a soul sister because I want my Afro washed and braided, except this one snow from Health, Education and Welfare— I taught her how to braid it. Or I might choose one because I want to make love in a certain way and this one makes love in this particular way better than the others.

"It's crazy. I'll tell you a funny thing that happened one night. I was coming down Sixteenth Street, coming toward East-West Highway, when I had to turn left if I was going to go see Betty Furstberg, my German monster in Georgetown, or I had to go right if I was going to go see this fine sister from Colorado, Melvina Pritchard.

"I was coming up on my turn and I still hadn't made up my mind. I started turning right, then I thought about Betty and turned back left, then I changed my mind and turned back right. I was so confused that I went straight, ran through a red light, and almost banged into the side of a Sloane's furniture truck." He laughs and shakes his head. "I was lucky that my Corvette has good brakes. I was lucky the road wasn't wet and slippery, man. I pulled to the side of the road and sat for a while, just thinking.

"But that doesn't mean I'm ruled by pussy. It's like being in New York—and this has actually happened to me too—I've been in New York and been hungry as hell but there were so many great restaurants around that I couldn't decide between Chinese, Italian, soul-food, French, uptown, downtown. I've been in that shape and have gone back to where I was staying without eating anything, because I didn't want to ruin the one hunger I had in just one restaurant. I couldn't have them all, so I didn't take any.

"That's what people have to understand about me. I'm not a pussy-crazy man. In fact, I can tell you this other story: One morning, last month it was, I met this lady—a white woman—in the park, and this will illustrate that I'm not dominated by pussy.

"I was out in the park jogging, looking pretty, jogging. Had on my long socks and shit, red-striped socks, running, working out, feeling good, sun shining. Early in the morning before time to go to work. Had a good night's sleep. My strides were good. My kicks were high. This woman came and started digging me, freaking out.

"'O-o-o-ow, I love bodies and you have such a nice body,' she said, but I remained totally different from what she had expected. I remained calm. I was of a different culture. I had ample ammunition to bombard her with, but I just turned around and jogged in one spot and said. 'Hi. How are you doing? Fine? Looks like you're outfitted for jogging; won't you join me?' She joined me. We jogged, jogged, talked, talked, jogged, and then I saw this other woman I knew, riding a bike. I called to her because I wanted to prolong this other woman's stay. I had used space against her by being from another culture, so now I want to put time on her. I want to see how much inconvenience she would endure, which is a true test of her intentions.

"So I started rapping to this other woman, just passing polite conversation. After a while the other woman said, 'I'm leaving.' That's all she said, 'I'm leaving,' but she was really thinking, 'I don't have to be subjected to this.'

"I said, 'Bye.' She went a little ways away and stopped. You have to dig what is happening. She's just met this black man, her social inferior. I've already put time and space on her, now I hit her with nonchalance—send her in the wind without looking around. She jogged a few paces away and turned and said, 'If you jog here often, perhaps we can jog again sometime. It was fun. See you here tomorrow.' Now, what does that sound like to you? This woman had never seen me before. What does that sound like?

"The next day, she was there waiting in approximately the same spot. I know; I drove past just to see if she was there, and she was there, stalling in the same spot. She was there, man. Didn't I see her with my own two eyes! Am I crazy? She was there. But I didn't get out of my car. I drove to another spot in the park and jogged. I waited until the next day. I came back to the spot where she was. I got out of the car and jogged over to her. 'Are you ready?' I asked.

"'Yes,' she said. 'Sorry I didn't make it yesterday.' I laughed. I know the games women play. We jog. On the way, she is talking. She tells me that she has a girl friend who has a West Indian boy friend. 'But he's much friendlier than you. You have an arrogant attitude.'

"I stop jogging. I look at her. I say, 'Hey, you don't even know me. I just met you. Don't tell me what fucking way to be.' I waited to see if she wanted to jog off. She just stood there. She dug it. She didn't like it but she had to dig it. What right did she have telling me how to behave? Plus, she being a Caucasian woman, telling me, a black man, how to behave?

"So for about three mornings she didn't show up. Then she showed up again. We jogged for several days without talking more than generalities. She was waiting for me to ask her for a formal date but I didn't ask. That was blowing her mind. Then, one evening, she called me. We talked. She invited me to a party, wanted to show me off. I knew it was time then to warm up to her. 'Thank you, thank you. That's very nice of you. You probably can't imagine how much I would like to go, but it just happens that I'm all tied up. Can we make it another night? Drinks after work perhaps? Oh, I wish I could come to the party. I wish you had told me earlier, I would have broken this engagement I have tonight. Can we get together next Wednesday for drinks?'

"She pauses, 'Wednesday is bad for me. Can we make it another night?'

"'Thursday? Any night you say.' I decide to give ground a little, give her pride a little something.

"'Thursday's fine, after work.' She gives me her number at work. I know that she doesn't have a damn thing to do Wednesday. She wants to play the same game I'm playing. I know women, man. That's why I can get so many of them. I know them and I think like they think.

Horn of Plenty   47

"That Thursday, I bring her back to my place after we have drinks at Bixby's. I have been very friendly to her all evening. Perfume, a token of my esteem. We come back to my place to listen to some records. We start off the evening lying on the floor, listening to Bob Marley, but when I go to get pillows for our heads she says, 'The bed is there, why don't we lie on the bed?'

"I said, 'If I had suggested that we lie on the bed, you would have thought bad of me, but since you mentioned it, why not lie on the bed?' So we get on the bed, side by side, listening to music. Side by side without touching. We lie there. All night she is twisting and turning. Her body wants me, you see, but her mind won't let her make the first move. She gets up and says, 'I must read,' or some other silly shit like that. 'I must do some reading for school.' She has a paperback book in her purse.

"She'd been reading all fucking day. She didn't want to read. She was taking this course at work and they kept her in school all fucking day. She didn't want to read, but she didn't want to make the first move either. I keep psyching her. I refuse to be aggressive with her. I just talk to her. I say, 'This is difficult for you, isn't it, and I'm not going to help you.'

"'What? . . . What are you talking about?' she says. She goes and reads for about a half hour, twitching and turning. I lie in the bed just like this, calm. She tiptoes around to see if I'm sleeping.

"I say, 'I'm not sleeping.'

"'Oh! I thought you were sleeping. I can't believe you've waited patiently all this time.'

"I said, 'I'm at home. I'm just lying here. I wasn't asleep. I was just lying here thinking.'

"So she lies back down on the bed, twisting and turning. 'You're a very strange man,' she says. In the wee hours of the morning, she reaches for me and I don't help her at all. She sits on the side of the bed and strokes my face.

"I say, 'I know this is very hard for you, a Caucasian woman offering yourself to a nigger and he being cool about it.'

"'No . . .' she says, 'but you really are a strange man.' She says she has to go. Then she wants to get out in a hurry. She gives me her telephone number at home. I walk her to the door. . . .

"Then there was this gorgeous devil from the World Bank. I knew her last year. Simply lovely. We were over to her girl friend's apartment one night and in walks Senator ————. He's drunk, or he would have called to make sure she was alone. He just took for granted that no one would be there, because she wouldn't have another man up there while Congress was in session, because the senator is paying all the bills and buying her things. He's got a lot of his clothing there, so it's obvious that he must sleep there some nights. A United States senator. You know him too. He's been on TV. You'd recognize him if I called him by name. From one of the western states. He's married. Kids. But he's supporting this woman. The three of us are there when he comes in: me, his woman, my woman. He's surprised.

"Of course he's surprised to see a nigger there, and my bitch is finer than his bitch, so he had to show off his money to come equal to me. He had to show off his power as a senator, but I can hold my own. We trade shots. He tries to impress me. I put music on that makes it hard for him to talk. I dance. I know he's digging my smoothness. Me up dancing by myself, both the women forgetting all about his talk and digging me doing my Reggae. My clothes fitting me nice. Smooth.

"I polish his ass off, you hear me. I polish his ass off. His life is dull compared to mine, and my bitch that I'm getting for free, better-looking than the one he's paying for. I dust him off.

"Sure, money is desirable, power is desirable. They can be powerful aphrodisiacs, but the money and power doesn't matter unless the money and power can help you get your personal thing off, whatever your thing happens to be. Of course, if I had his money I would be able to get my thing off better, bigger, but I do okay. My shit shines. Believe me. He knew it.

"Just for spite I thought about doubling back and loving his

Horn of Plenty   49

lady, but my lady asked me not to do that. I asked her, 'Why? Don't you want your friend to have some of the good thing you've had? She's your best friend.'

"My lady said, 'I'm scared. You might like her more than you like me. No, please don't. She's attracted to you. She's said so. And she *would* make love to you just to spite me, even if she *wasn't* attracted. She's been going with Senator ————, so she's always had something up on me. Now I've got something up on her. I don't want her to taste you,' my lady said.

"So you see how women think. I argued with her the whole night trying to talk her into approving of me making a hit on her friend. Tease her friend, give it to her once and then refuse to give it to her again. Make my lady even prouder. But I couldn't get my lady to do it. But I did almost talk her into it. So you see how women think? I know them. And I know the senator tried to arrange a date between my lady and one of his friends. My lady told me. She come asking me, 'Can I go out with his friend?' I said, 'Yes, go ahead.'

"She said, 'You must not love me.'

"I said, 'On the contrary, I love you very much. I love you and want the best for you.' And that was an honest expression of my feelings. I did care a great deal about her. She was one of the kindest, most generous people I knew. She cared about me. Not just as a sex object but as a person. She loved me. I know that. But I never get things confused. When it came time for her to do what she had to do, she would leave me, as she subsequently did. I don't see her any more. She moved into another phase of her life. She moved over into the lily-white suburbs in Virginia.

"She dates marriageable junior wheeler-dealers on their way up. If one fails she'll divorce him and marry another one. I don't fault her for this. That's what I think about love. It has to fit in with what you want out of life. If you're a smart person. Love, man, love is intelligent, well-directed affection.

"But if you want to talk about the completely irrational side of it. Yes, I could say that there was one relationship that actually stands above the others"; his voice grows soft. "I give it that importance only because I want to give it that emphasis.

"Why am I so reluctant to talk about the serious side of

love? I've been talking about the serious side all along. It's all serious. This one I mention as different from the others only because it was the first time I had ever had feelings like this about another person. I was eighteen. She was fifteen, Charlotte Jennings. We were in high school together. We were in love together.

"I could say I loved her more than I loved any other woman. I could say that if *I* wanted to place that value on it. Or I could say it was primarily a sex thing, but I don't think it was. The sex thing was very intense, but it was love, too. It was so strong it was frightening. It had me running around in a circle. I didn't know what to do. I couldn't get this woman out of my blood. As young as she was, she had this hold on me. Fifteen, man.

"I used to hurt when I wasn't around her, and when I was around her all I wanted to do was touch her or make love to her. I used to borrow her uncle's car and we would drive out somewhere in Maryland and make love. I used to make love to her on the floor in her mother's living room with her mother right upstairs. Her parents knew what was going on but they were smart enough to know that it had to go on. One time, I made love to her so hard she fainted. She was in a trance. I was scared as hell. She wasn't moving. It was about a half hour before I could revive her. We made love standing up.

"I mean she would say that it was time for her to go up-stairs and we would start to moving toward the stairs but I would make love to her again in the hallway before I went out the door home. That was a woman I didn't want to lose, but at the same time I was developing this fabulous rapport with her cousin. With her cousin it wasn't a sexual thing, but there was this fabulous mental thing that we were developing. I was screwing her cousin but it wasn't that great. I found her somewhat frigid, sexually cold, but emotionally very warm, generous, giving.

"I'm not trying to make an excuse for myself. I know I was wrong for loving two cousins at the same time, but at that period in my life I would have made love to her mother if I had gotten the chance.

"But in my youth, in my ignorance, I thought that me and

Horn of Plenty   51

Charlotte had such a fantastic copulation going that she would never go with another man. But she did. Not because she wanted to, but because she suspected that I was going with her cousin. She didn't know, she just suspected, and so she went with this other man to hurt me.

"It hurt me. It hurt me very much, but you know it made me a little joyful, too. I hurt for a long time, but I was happy that I was hurting, because I learned from that. It took me about two years to get over that hurt completely, but all that time I was learning that no matter how much a woman says she loves you, if she sees something else she wants she'll go and get it.

"I was thankful for that, because it taught me to be self-contained. I learned not to be ruled by this copulation. From that I learned never to be angry at a woman no matter what she does, because if she knows that something will make you angry she'll use that against you. Like this woman Charlotte Jennings. She told me all the details of her affair with this other man. She did this just to hurt me.

"I remember how it happened. We were in Rock Creek Park. She told me she had known about me and her cousin for a long time. Then she told me about this other man. She just picked out this occasion to tell me everything. She said, 'You jive motherfucker, you low-down motherfucker.' We were at a picnic. I was eating this hot dog, drinking this cola. I was petrified by her telling this to me. She was overexcited. People were gathering. I said, 'Charlotte, stop telling me this; cool yourself.'

"I told her if she kept this up I was going to have to do something to her, but she continued. She came in my face, 'You stinking motherfucker!' So I threw the cola in her face—bam! Hot dog in her face—bam! Slapped her—bam! The cola trickled down and she just smiled. She said, 'O-o-o-ow, I got you, didn't I? O-o-o-ow, I got you!' She just loved it.

"So I learned from that. I'm not so quick to slap a woman now. Like this other woman. I was going with her. I caught her one day fucking this other dude. She was supposed to be my lady. I caught her in the act, man. In my place, but I didn't aggress her. I said, 'You're not even worth beating.' She looked like a little dog. She stood there like a little dog. I preferred that. I learned to be above hurt. That's why I can do what I do with women.

"And this doesn't mean that I hate women. I love women. I love them, man. I'm happy, man. I know now that I can have women when I want them and then not have them when I don't want them, and when I don't have them it's because that's what *I* choose. I'm not lonely when I don't have them.

"And I'm not saying that I can get any woman I want, but every woman who comes into my vibration has to react to me. If it's nothing more than to say to herself, register within herself, 'I don't want him.' That's the kind of vibration I send out —a very sensual vibration that makes a woman make a sexual decision. Even the cologne I wear along with my natural aura forces a sexual decision, which isn't always in my favor.

"Some women might not open up to me because they feel that I have too many women already. That's true. I've been to parties where each woman there thought that I was interested in the other woman, so she wouldn't expose herself to the possibility of rejection, while in reality I didn't even have a woman at the time.

"See, all that does is reflect on a woman's own insecurities. She thinks that I would not choose her, because she feels within herself that she's not as attractive as some other women there. It's true.

"Or I might start to dig a chick and she just take for granted: 'I know he's got a lot of women so I'm not going to have anything to do with him . . . he's . . . he's . . . he's handsome and all that but I'll just watch him. If he says anything to me it will be a pleasure to turn him down. I really don't want to but I have to,'" He laughs. "That's true, man. That's true. Women do that to me," he said, slumping deep, stretching his long body out across the white vinyl-covered beanbag chair.

4

Jamundo

And it really takes that long to heal?

"They'll ruin your life, all those old West Indian women," Sandra said. "When my mother found out I was in love, she threatened to send me back to St. Croix. She said she would tell the Immigration I had done something wrong and that I should go back to live with my grandmother in the Virgin Islands. And I would go, too. I'm not very rebellious. I would probably go," Sandra said. A smile crossed her smooth, jet-black, boyish face.

"That's why I don't know if I was in love or not. I don't know," she fretted. "How could I really be in love if I gave him up the first time my mother threatened me? I didn't fight for him. She couldn't send me back to the West Indies. I'm twenty-one, you know, yeas, mahn. I'm a citizen. Love is something you fight for, isn't it?

"But those old women, they can get inside your head, you know. They can tell you things. They can tell you, you don't love this boy—this Jamundo. What is love, child? You don't know what love is. What is love?" Sandra asked herself. "The man who invented love, they should detain him. They should put him in jail and throw away the key." She laughed, but not loud enough for her mother to hear.

"But I think I did love Jamundo. I used to dream about him. He's a very sexy little fellow, you know. He doesn't wear underwears, yes, underwear. He had a little beard and soft shoes that make him look like a little elf." When she laughed, her eyes sparkled as white as her straight, white teeth.

"I guess the main thing is he's so different. He always says unusual things, and he likes weird stuff: weird jazz and abstract art. And I guess one other reason why I like him is I knew my mother wouldn't like him." She stretched lazily on the green cellophane-covered sofa and looked toward the kitchen, where her mother was. "But Mother fooled me. At first she like him. Yes, at first she liked him."

Sandra was playing a game with her mother, saying things almost loud enough for her mother to hear. She enjoyed the game as if it were the only revenge she could take on the matriarch busy washing dishes in the kitchen. Sandra is no more rebellious than that. She looks much younger than twenty-one in her unfamiliar Afro. This June, she will graduate from City College with a B.S. in biology. "What is love?" she asked.

"I don't know," I said.

"But you're doing the book on it. You should know." Sandra's body, though thin, is round, indication that in time she might fatten out like her mother. Her mother is the kind of plump, dark West Indian woman who makes you think of good, spicy food and warm laughter, but she didn't laugh or even smile very much at the stranger who had come to talk to her youngest daughter about this thing, this foolish, foolish thing, love.

"We can't talk here," Sandra said as her mother passed, for the third time, through the neat little living room where we were sitting. "We can go to the park. Let's go to the park and talk. I'm interested. I'm really interested. I want to know about this mysterious thing."

We went down through the dim hallway into the outdoors. The sun was low but still brightly shining down the street from the far end. We walked toward it. "My mother is mad at you. Oh-h-h, is she mad at you! She doesn't like American men anyway," Sandra laughed. "She doesn't. She says they're no good. Is that true?"

"I don't know."

She walked sideways, talking. The park was crowded with people who had come out to sit after supper. Old Jewish men and women occupied most of the benches. The newcomers to the neighborhood, younger West Indians, lounged on the grass or sat on the railings that ran along parts of the walkway.

"One more month of school," I said.

"Yes; I'm really frightened about love, though. Love is a very cruel thing, you know. This Jamundo— I told him I never wanted to see him again," she said, still walking sideways. "But suppose I love him. Suppose I love him and never see him again. I walk around the house now thinking about him. I can't eat. I can't sleep. Suppose I love him? Oh, my God. How did I get myself into this?

"You know, I used to think when I got twenty-one I could

go and do what I wanted. But that's not true. I find I'm still living by my mother's rules. Why won't she let me go? That's terrible." We sat in the shade, since only shaded benches were vacant. The old Jews preferred to warm and tan themselves in the dying sun.

"This boy Jamundo. He's my age. He's twenty-two. Maybe that's the problem. I need an older man, a much older man. I've always been attracted to older men, you know, really! I've always liked older men, but this boy—last night I dreamed of him, yes! He has me so upset." She sucked at the roof of her mouth, making a clicking sound that expressed her exasperation.

"When I come home from school in the evening, all I do is think about him. I can't concentrate on anything but him. But I don't want him back. I want it to be over, once and for all. That's what I want. Perhaps my mother was right. He only wants to marry me to get his citizenship. He's a Trinidadian. A little skinny Trinny, you know." She laughed at her rhyme. "They're like that, you know. They have to marry an American citizen to get the citizenship.

"Perhaps that's why. But he says he doesn't want to marry me. He wants me to live with him. Oh, my God! I couldn't live with a man without being married. My mother would die," she said, quarreling with herself.

"He treats me like he's my father. These West Indian men, they're very strict on their women, but they're very free themselves. In the West Indies many of them have children by outside women. It's very unfair. Jamundo, he has a child. Yes! A child by another woman, but he's very jealous of me. These West Indian men, they will kill for that thing. He told me if he saw me with another man he would smack me down. He would do it, too." She laughed and shook her head.

"Maybe I've never been in love. I think I'm afraid of love. It's like it says in that book by Gibran: 'Even as love crowns you, it will crucify you.' I guess that's what I'm most afraid of, that love will bring me down. No, my heart is not more delicate than anyone else's. I wouldn't commit suicide or anything like that. I would recover, but someone would have to help me, I swear, and there's no one to help. I have no one to talk to. I couldn't talk to my mother. My brother would laugh at me. He would—" she laughed. "He would laugh at me."

"What might happen is I would dislike men for a long time. If I got hurt bad I would freeze up for a long time, and I'm afraid of that." She began to sweat a little on her nose. Old folks say that evil people sweat on the nose. I imagined that she did have a bad temper when she let loose. I bet she did give that little "skinny Trinny" hell. The soft wind did not dry her little-boy nose. She rubbed it with long, bony fingers. A red-stone ring flashed on one of them.

The sun had gone down but daylight remained. She continued to talk. Her voice was full of caution, and sometimes it grew so soft that I had to look down at the needle on the tape recorder to make sure it was picking up what she was saying. Transcribing the soft parts of her conversation would be difficult, I thought, and no one could help with this, since I always used the time while transcribing to arrange some of the random comments into a flowing narrative.

Much of what she said was similar to things I had heard, but I didn't mind that. The book needed lines of conversation that had the familiarity of ritual. Fear was at the center of her ritual. She was afraid, and she had every right to be. Who could tell what Jamundo, any Jamundo, was up to? Who could be absolutely sure?

But she enjoyed talking about love. Her interest in it gave her a nervous kind of energy that made her eyes twinkle and her body jerk playfully.

"I was very happy as a child in St. Croix," she said. "Childhood was very nice. I was very happy. How can you be unhappy when you don't have a mind of your own? How can you? You can't," she said. A little woman with bouncy hair was using the park as a short cut home from work. She came past us and smiled. She didn't speak, but her lips moved as if to say hello. Sandra knew her. She lived on the second floor of Sandra's building.

"I didn't think for myself. I was happy doing what I was told. I was born in a little house in Frederiksted, which is at the far end of the island. It was in a town, in a way, but even at that it was very rural, with the goats running the streets and all. Not like New York.

"We were very poor. I remember that, but most of the people in St. Croix were poor, so it didn't matter as much. Before that, my mother's first husband had run off to Antigua with an Antiguan woman. That's the way the men do down there. They don't need a divorce. No. All they do is run to another island. Her first husband was a pistol; he gave her a fit while he was with her." Sandra stopped talking and pointed down the walkway. "See that little boy on the red bike? He lives next door to us. My mother sent him out to watch me. 'Go looka Sandra. See where she be.' My mother's like that.

There was no doubt that the little dark boy was watching us. It was funny how he tried to pretend that he was just kneeling there fixing his bike. "If I wanted to I could go away with you. All I have to do is give him a quarter and he wouldn't tell on me."

I laughed. "He comes pretty cheap for a double agent."

"Anyway, my mother's first husband left her with two children. He just took off and left. She never heard from him again. She was very bitter against men for a long time. I hear that any man who came around her had hell to pay.

"In two years she met my father and he married her. I was born soon after then. My mother and father loved each other very much, but we had many hardships because we were very poor.

"My father worked very hard. He was a tobacco stripper. It was hard work and it didn't pay much, but he was so old-fashioned that he didn't want his wife to work. He was from the old school. He thought that a woman should be home with the kids." The dark boy stopped fixing his bike and rode a little closer to us. No doubt he was coming close to see if Sandra wanted to call him in for a bribe. Sandra only smiled when I nodded for her to notice him. She was lost in remembering.

"The happiest day of my life was when I started school. I was very tall for my age, and I had learned the ABC's and I could count to a hundred before I was five years old, so my mother lied about my age. Most of the other kids were six or seven. I was the only five-year-old in the first grade. I was very proud of that.

"I was a good child, you know. I was. I was proud because my mother would say: 'Looka Sandra, she's only five and she can read.' Neither of my parents could read." The little dark boy finally rode over to us and asked Sandra if she wanted him to go to the store for her. I wanted a beer, but I knew he couldn't buy it. We ordered sodas. I gave him a dollar and he rode away.

"And another thing. I was the first child of my mother's love for my father. The man she married first, I don't think she loved him, but my father she really loved. That's what happened, I think. I think she loved him too much. See, if you love too much that's bad also.

"Anyway, I guess you could say that I was the favorite, but they were very strict on me. My mother was a Methodist and she was very strict. And I wanted to please her. I knew if I was clean, for instance, it would please my mother, so I would always stay clean for her. I came home from school as clean as I went. Yes, even if I were wearing white I would come home spotless.

"Whatever my parents told me to do, I would do and never question it. If I had a friend at school and my mother would dislike my friend, I would give up that friend. I didn't go out to play much, because my mother didn't want me to get dirty and she didn't want me to get my legs all scarred up, so I sat in the house most of the time. I didn't miss having fun as a kid. I didn't miss it until I got older and thought back on it," she said.

"Now I see kids playing with the Johnny pump and I ask myself why I didn't play much as a kid. They go in under the water and they laugh. I missed things like that. In one sense, I never had a childhood.

"But how can you be unhappy if you don't have a mind of your own? I didn't think about boys and I certainly didn't think about love. I did dream about getting married. I always dreamed about getting dressed all in white and going to the church. I think all girls have that dream.

"My other dreams came from books. I read a lot. I could read better than anyone in my family, so my older sister had to do all the housework. I came home and I was free to read. My mother would say: 'You study the books and someday you'll be very smart and make lots of money. You'll go to college and meet the right man and he'll get a woman to do the housework for you.'

"Then, when I was twelve, my father died. That changed everything. He died very foolishly. He was at work and he had this pain, and the place where he worked was near his mother's house, so he went to her house to complain about the pain. She was old; she didn't know. She gave him a laxative and it turned out that he had appendicitis and you're not supposed to give a laxative to someone who has appendicitis. But my grandmother was very old; she didn't know this. He died before they got him to the hospital.

"After that, our whole life changed. My mother had to go to work. I could now run in the streets more, but I didn't want to. My older brother tried to take over for my father, but he was only fifteen. I think the problem was that my mother loved my father too much. She would say: 'He was a good man, Sandra. There aren't very many like him. It's like looking for a needle in a haystack. Your father was a good man,' she would say.

"I think right now she would like me to marry a man like my father. No, not exactly like him, because he was poor and uneducated, but like him. I think it was less than a year after he died that we came to New York, which was the biggest mistake we ever made. But I'm glad we did. If I was in St. Croix I would be married now, with children, and fat. I would be a woman now." She laughed. "It's true, you know. I would be a woman and not a virgin. Can you imagine that, a twenty-one-year-old virgin? Oh, my God," she laughed.

"I remember one day before we left. It was on my birthday. I had just turned thirteen and it so happened that my birthday fell on Election Day, and so there was a lot of fireworks and music and celebrating. It was nice, like a small carnival. Delroy Comfort's Calypso Band was playing. I remember that because Delroy Comfort wanted to talk to my sister but my mother wouldn't allow it. A musician? Never. Anyway, a bunch of kids were playing away from the celebration, but it wasn't far, because I remember we could hear the music and laughing.

"That night, this little boy was chasing me, asking me if I wanted him to make a real woman out of me. And for some reason I had the hottest feeling for this crazy little boy. He was chasing me and trying to accidentally feel on me as we wrestled. He chased me down a dark road. He was a crazy little boy. I think he must have been about fourteen. I had never liked him, but that day I felt very warm toward him. He caught me in the bushes and I was ready to give in to him when my cousin came along and ran him away.

"So you see, when I left St. Croix I was ready to become a woman. I was ready to love. But when I got to New York, I felt like such a little girl. All my sexual feelings went away," she said.

"Coming to New York was very bad for us, you know. Everything happened. . . . Part of my problem was my sister. I saw what my sister went through with men and that frightened me. I began to put a shell around myself, trying to protect myself."

The dark boy brought our sodas back from the store. He didn't say anything about change, so I didn't mention it.

"Anyway, when we came to New York we had to stay with my Auntie. She was married and had a son, so there were eight of us in a five-room apartment. And on top of that, my mother and Auntie were always arguing. They couldn't get along.

"Then my sister fell in love with a guy. She really loved him, but he was married and we didn't know it. Men are terrible, you know. He went back to his wife, and my sister went to the top of the apartment building and jumped off—five stories. This happened the first year we came to New York. She didn't kill herself, but she had to stay in the hospital for almost a year. The guy never came to the hospital once to see her.

"Right now she walks with a limp because of that. And for two years she never told us why she jumped off the roof. What happened was the guy had gotten her pregnant and she was too ashamed to tell us, so she tried to kill herself before we found out. We never would have found out if the guy hadn't left his wife and tried to come back to her. Then she told us what had happened," she said. The little boy got tired of watching and took his bike inside.

"After that, I was afraid of love. We lived in a horrible neighborhood in Manhattan. There wasn't a lot of dope in the block then, but there were a lot of winos. I used to watch them from the window. I would never go down in the street unless I was going to school or to the store or something. But what I used to see from that window, it would make me afraid. I saw women and men fighting all the time, so I didn't want to think about love. I could never go out. I could never meet boys. The only time we went out was as a family. At school I hung around with a group of West Indian girls who didn't worry about boys and partying and that sort of stuff. The American children didn't like us. The black Americans were worst. They called us such names. I had never been called names like that before—coconut, black Jews, monkey-huggers—I had never been called such names.

"But along about then, I think, I began to feel my sexual nature. It wasn't as strong as it was back in St. Croix, but it was strong. I began noticing boys. In the eleventh grade there was this very black boy in my class. I couldn't keep my eyes off him. I couldn't. Of course he never knew I was watching him, but I watched this boy. He was so handsome. I think I loved that boy for the whole year without saying a word to him. I was afraid.

"I knew my mother would die if I brought this boy home. He was an American. I wouldn't bring him home because I knew what Ma would say. Right now, I can't even buy a new dress for worrying about what my mother will say. When I'm at school dancing, I can feel her eyes burning into me. She makes you afraid. She tells you that men will use you and drop you. I'm supposed to be a very sexy sign, according to astrology—at least that's what I'm reading about Scorpio—but I don't know if I am, you know.

"I wish my mother would read that part in *The Prophet* about children. Have you read it?"

"No," I said.

"It says: 'Your children are not your children. They are sons and daughters of life's longing for itself. They come through you but not from you. They are of you but they do not belong to you.' She should read that."

"You read a lot of poetry?" I asked.

"I like very sad poems. I like love poems," she laughed.

"Have you ever tried to bring a boy friend home?"

"Yes, of course, Jamundo, he knows my mother."

"I mean, did you ever try to bring any other boy friends home?"

"Are you kidding! I wouldn't dare. Yes, I did. In my senior year of high school I was terribly attracted to this older man, so I would meet him after school or at the grocery store. Then, one day, I decided to bring him home to meet my mother. It was so embarrassing. She went on and on telling him that I didn't need a boy friend and that I had to finish my education. She told him never to come back to her house. She did! Right to his face. I almost died.

"She is so afraid. She is so afraid, that she makes me afraid. She dislikes every man that I'm interested in. But at first she liked Jamundo. The first time he came to my house, he was very impressive, with bow tie and all. He kissed my mother's hand. He flattered her. She was very impressed. Everything was all right. My mother is prejudiced. She really is. She doesn't like American blacks and she doesn't like West Indians from other places. She liked Jamundo until she found out he was from Trinidad. Then she started telling me that he only wanted to marry me to get his citizenship.

"She kept saying 'Not him, Sandra. You mustn't marry him. Those Trinidadians. They're no good. They drink. They hit their women. They will marry you to get the citizenship, then they will leave.' I couldn't tell her that he didn't want to marry me. He wanted to live with me without being married. But do you know what? I started believing that he was after me because of the citizenship thing, like my mother said. That's how strong her influence is on me.

"Why did I do that? I knew it wasn't true. I knew he loved me. He couldn't do without me. He couldn't go a day without calling me. I knew he loved me, but one day I called him over to my house and I told him, 'I never want to see you again, Jamundo!' I said it very boldly.

"He said, 'Why, Sandra, why?' He was really hurt." She laughed.

"I said, 'I don't owe you an explanation. Make this the last time I see you, Jamundo.'

"A tear came to his eye. 'At least you could tell me why. What have I done? Have I insulted your mother?'

"I said, 'No, I just don't want to see you again.' I was very cruel. He started to cry. I said, 'Don't cry. Take it like a man, all right?' I was very cold.

"After he left, my mother came into the room. She asked, 'Sandra, child, what's wrong with Jamundo?'

"I said, 'I just quit Jamundo, Mother.'

"She looked at me and she had this beautiful look on her face."

5
Day of Furious Intent

If, by love, that's what you mean, then yes, I was once in love.

There was a slyness about the smile that wrinkled the corners of her narrow lips. She is Puerto Rican, light, with jet-black hair. "I was very confused then," she said. "I didn't know what I thought at the time, but I can tell you about it. I was young then. I was only twenty-one. I know this much: I know it gave me a funny feeling to be around him. I liked it and I didn't like this feeling it gave me. There were times when I was eager to get to work to see him, and other times when I thought about quitting my job and never coming back.

"Maybe I *was* in love. Maybe that was love. I know it was different from anything I've ever felt before or since. At first I think I did hate him. I hated him because he was black. For one thing, I didn't like the way he looked at me. Every day when I came to work, I was nervous because I knew this man was going to look at me. There was no way to stop him from looking at me, but it made me hate him and think of him as dirt.

"I can't describe how he looked at me. He looked at me not like he was looking at me but like he was looking through me. He looked inside me, seeing something I was hiding. I think he had no right to do this. He was my boss, so I had to talk to him. I could tell that he was nervous when he talked to me. We could barely talk to each other because of mutual nervousness. What I hated was the idea that he might have that I was nervous because I liked him.

"This place we worked was a credit-checking bureau. He was a division manager and there were about eight girls working under him, making telephone contacts with different accounts. After we made a dozen or so calls we had to go into his office and discuss them with him and he would tell us what to do on each account.

"The other girls—their accounts were no tougher than mine, but they spent more time in his office with him. He laughed and joked with them and made chitchat. Sometimes he closed the door with one of them in there, and you could see them laughing through the glass. Or you could see the girl telling him her problems, personal problems.

"The other girls liked him very much. He was very handsome and very young to be a supervisor. Whenever I went into his office, there was always this nervousness. He never laughed and joked. We said what we had to say to each other and I left.

"One of the reasons why I hated him was because he was very much in love with himself. I hate people who are conceited. He had all these girls admiring him, so he thought he was hot stuff. I hate people who think they are superior. I was aching for an opportunity to tell him that he was no better than anyone else.

"I was waiting for him to make me mad so I could tell him. Actually I have a very bad temper and all I needed was half a chance. I know that he didn't know this. I know that he thought that I liked him. That's the main thing I disliked about him.

"He was handsome in a way, but he certainly was no better-looking than my husband. I had just gotten married the year before. I was happily married, but at home sometimes I would think about my boss and this arrogant attitude he had.

"My husband is nice. I love him. I loved him then very much. I was reared a Catholic. I am very strict. My parents were not strict Catholics. This strictness was something I took on myself. Something that resulted from my own personality. In fact I spent two months in a monastery because I thought for a while that I wanted to be a nun.

"I stayed there two months and then I decided that I wanted to do something else. Marriage was like that for me. I loved my husband but I had the feeling that I wanted to do something else.

"I think I got married just because I had sexual needs and I knew that being married was the only way I could satisfy them without feeling guilty. I feel guilty very easily. So, you know, I felt guilty about the way this man, my boss, looked at me.

"My husband was satisfying me sexually. It wasn't that. It was just that I wanted something else. I don't know what. I didn't have someone else specifically in mind that I wanted. It wasn't sexual. It was something inside me. Something emotional. Maybe it was because I had gotten married too young.

"I used to think about my boss. He was fair to me. He didn't give me any more work than he gave the other girls, but he treated me different than the other girls. There was something different in the way he treated me. I resented that. I resented him, but at the same time I was very attracted to him. I had begun to think of him all the time at home. My husband didn't know what was wrong with me. He asked my mother, 'Mrs. Hernández, what's wrong with Iris?' My mother didn't tell him, but she remembered an incident in my childhood that told her what was wrong with me. She began to side with him. She began to feel sorry for him. She told him that any time I wouldn't cook he could come to her house to eat. She got very close to him. I hated her for that. Me and my mother had never been close since the time I was a child.

"When I was a child she used to tell me that I had the eyes of a *puta*, which in Spanish is a whore. She said I had the sneaky eyes of a whore. As a teen-ager, my sisters would not bring their husbands or boy friends around me, because they said I had this manner of a *puta*. That I had these eyes that looked like a *puta*'s eyes, and their boy friend would always want to talk to me.

"I knew that my boss was seeing this same thing in me. It was not only the way he looked at me but the way he refused to look at me sometimes, the way he ignored me for no reason, the way he was nervous when he talked to me, and he never closed the door when I went into his office. I resented this.

"He didn't know I resented it. He knew I was nervous around him, but he probably thought it was because I liked him. I hated for him to think that. I hated him, because his skin was black and mine was white. I wondered could he see this, and did this make him want me more.

"One night in winter, he took all of the girls in the office out for drinks after work, to celebrate this one girl's birthday. I remember it was winter, because it was almost dark when we left the office. We went to this place called The Coachman, and we were all sitting around talking. He, being the only man, was of course the center of attention. I hated that. He was a good conversationalist, and he was keeping us all entertained, and he was the kind of person who was careful to say something nice about each girl. He started talking about what he considered to be the outstanding feature of each girl's personality.

"He would say that this girl was the most practical girl in the office, and this one was the most idealistic, and this one was the most ambitious, and this one was the most wifely. I was very afraid of what he was going to say about me. He started with the girl next to me and went around the table in the opposite direction, saving me for last. He kept saying a little something about each girl and we, or they, would all laugh about it and comment on it. I didn't say anything. The closer he got to me the more nervous I became.

"Then he told the girl just before me that she was the most sensual person in the office.

"By that time everyone was looking at me. 'You could never guess. She's so quiet you could never guess.' He was looking at me, smiling. I smiled. He thought I approved of what he was saying, but actually his laughter made me sick. Everyone had stopped laughing and they were all looking at me.

"'You know how you can tell? Look at her eyes,' he said. I knew that the only reason he had the courage to say this to me was because all the other girls were there. He didn't have the courage to say anything like that to me when we were alone in his office. 'She is the sexiest woman in the office,'" he said.

"I realized for the first time that he was afraid of me, but this did not make me sympathetic to him. It made me despise him even more. He had no right to say that to me, and so I knew I had to tell him everything that had been on my mind since the first time I saw him. I had to tell him that I had hated him from the first day I came on the job. I had started not to take the job. I thought of asking for a transfer, that first day, to another department.

"I am not very sexy at all. I enjoy making love to my husband. My husband says I am very sexy, but I don't feel very sexy. For two days after this incident I didn't return to work. Actually the incident took place on a Friday, so I didn't come to work the following Monday or Tuesday. I stayed shut up in my room for all this time.

"My husband loves making love to me, and I love making love to him. Even if I wasn't married, I wouldn't make love to my boss.

"My life has never been under my control. I really wanted to quit my job. There was no one I could talk to about this. Actually the only one I felt would understand was my boss. He was the only one I knew who could understand. You could tell by his eyes that he really understood women, that he could understand me.

"I was born in Puerto Rico in the country, not in San Juan. I was a peasant girl, as they say. The first boy I ever really loved was a black, not a black American like my boss, but a black Puerto Rican. I think I loved this boy too much. No I didn't make love to him. I was a virgin when I got married, and I was only thirteen when I loved this boy, and he was only eleven, skinny and very black.

"I loved him. I really loved him. In Puerto Rico, skin color means a different thing than in the States.

"Maybe I never got over the fact that this black boy left me, especially since I thought I was better than him, and I would have defied my family to be with him. My mother had told my brothers to beat him up if they ever saw him coming around me. He left me for a girl who was lighter than I was, a Puerto Rican who was very fair-skinned.

"I could never let my boss make love to me. There were three reasons. First, I was married. Second, I would have felt even stranger coming to work each day and seeing him, and third, I could never make love to a black man. I could never marry a black man.

"I wanted to tell my boss all three of these reasons. I knew it would be hard to tell him, especially since he didn't take up time with me.

"I don't think I'm ugly, but I am not the most beautiful girl in the office. Some of the black girls are very nice. Some of the white girls are very nice. There is another Puerto Rican girl, who sits closer to his office, who is very nice. Then, why did he want me? I wondered. I'm very plain. Since coming to the states, I have put on weight. In Puerto Rico I weighed 107; now I weigh 137.

"If I were not married and he wasn't black, I would have been very attracted to him. There is something nice-looking about him. He's slender. I used to watch him when he wasn't looking my way. He really didn't act conceited all the time. He worked very hard. He made good money and he was sure to move up in the company. I didn't know it at the time, but I was probably having a nervous breakdown. It happens to a lot of people who come to this country and have to fit into the system here.

"Back then, there were times when my English got confused with Spanish, and one day one of my accounts called my boss to complain about me. He told my boss that the company should hire people who speak English. This happened on a Friday morning, so toward the end of the day my boss called me in to tell me about it.

"I sat down in the chair beside his desk. I was nervous, because I knew that I was going to tell him all that had been on my mind for so long.

"This man who had called complaining about me—my boss told me that he had cursed the man out and the man had called his *boss* and that his boss had called him in, and he had reminded his boss that he ran a good department and that he wanted to handle the matter in his own way.

"My boss was speaking very casually. He knew he was not going to get fired. He was too valuable to the company, and I knew that I had nothing to fear, because he would not let his boss fire me.

"Finally he said that if the guy didn't like the way I spoke he could take his business somewhere else. I told my boss I was sorry I got him into hot water. He said, 'Sh-i-i-t, don't be sorry, nothing's gon happen to me.'

"I hate men who curse. I hate for them to curse in front of

me, disrespecting me. What right did he have? I have never cursed in front of him. I do not use such words, ever. I remember the night he took all the girls out. He had said that it was between me and this other girl as to who was the most sympathetic person in the office. I am not very sympathetic. I am very critical of other people. Since coming to the States, I have few friends. Most people, I instantly start to dislike, for reasons I don't know. I'm a very confused person. I can't stick to a schedule. I can never get my life in order. Yet I'm a perfectionist where others are concerned. I am forever finding fault with my husband. Even if I learn not to say bad things to him, I still think them. I don't see how he lives with me. And my boss, while his appearance is very neat and he has nice clothes, which he wears well, his desk is always a mess. I was annoyed by the papers strewn everywhere and the rings on the surface of his desk where he had placed his coffee cup without bothering to use a saucer.

"There was no reason why he should ruin a desk like that, especially a desk that didn't belong to him but to the company. Between words I cut him off and told him that he should clear his desk a little better. He took this as a joke. He started talking about the job again, and when my mind wandered off again he asked, 'Do you like your job?'

"Very bluntly, I said, 'No. I hate it.'

"He was shocked. 'You hate it?' He didn't know what to say. " 'Why?'

" 'I don't know. I hate my job. I've always hated it.'

" 'Is the work too hard?'

" 'It's not the work,' I said staring at him for a moment, then dropping my eyes.

" 'Does everyone treat you all right?'

" 'Yes.'

" 'Do you like the other girls in the office," he asked.

"I felt my courage leaving me. I didn't know if I could go through with it, so I decided to lie. 'Yes, it's the other girls. Shelly is an idiot. Brenda— I hate people like that.' I hated myself for saying this. True, Shelly was an idiot and I don't

Day of Furious Intent   77

like people like Brenda, who try to get ahead by playing up to people, but I hated myself because I had started to tell him about him and then my courage had left me.

"'Is it something else?' he asked. I was sure now that he knew me and was not going to let me off. I felt cornered. 'Is it something else?' He got up and closed the office door. I didn't look through the glass to see if the other girls noticed, but I had the feeling that they were all staring through the glass at my back as they put on their coats to go home. I couldn't look up to meet his eyes. 'Do you think I'm a bad supervisor?'

"'Yes. I don't like the way you run the department,' I said.

"'Well, my method works,' he said. 'Ask the people I work for.'

"'It's just something about the way you do things,' I said.

"'How?'

"'You're a very sloppy person,' I said. 'You should clear up your desk.'

"'Do you want a transfer?'

"'I think I'll quit my job,' I said. I had to say something, and once I said that I would quit I felt very good. I felt courageous again. I told him about the night he had said I was the sexiest girl in the office. I told him that I had hated him since then.

"'I'm sorry to hear that. You shoulda tole me long time ago. I coulda retracted that. I was just making conversation. It didn't mean that damn much to me,' he said with a touch of anger in his voice.

"'Yes, I shoulda told you. I wanted to tell you, but I was always afraid, because I didn't like the way you looked at me.'

"He stared without saying anything. I brought my eyes up to meet his. 'How do I look at you?'

"'I don't know how to say. My English is not good,' I said, hiding behind this excuse and instantly feeling ashamed.

"'I have no idea what you're talking about,' he said. He was lying, too. He knew what I meant. He just wanted me to say it.

"'You look at me different than you look at the other girls.'

"'Do I?'

"I looked around and the office was empty beyond his door. The outer door was closed, but I could see through the high window that the hallway was dark. 'Yes.'

" 'How does it make you feel? Good or bad?'

"I knew he wanted me to say good, so I said bad. It did make me feel bad and cheap.

" 'You sure it makes you feel bad?' he said. I could feel that he was pursuing me.

" 'I don't know how to say it. My English is not good to say all that is on my mind.' I said something to him in Spanish. Then I said in English, 'From the first time I saw you I hated you.'

" 'Am I ugly?'

" 'You're okay,' I said. I wasn't going to give him any reassurance. 'But it's not because of what you look like, what your physical features are. You have pleasant facial features. It's something else.'

" 'What, then?' he asked cautiously.

"I wondered if I was hurting him. I wanted to hurt him bad. I stared at him for a long time. This was the first time I could stare at him for a long time without looking away.

" 'It looks bad, us sitting in here alone after hours. Let's go to my place and finish talking. I'm glad you're being frank. Believe me, I am.'

"Even though I was married, I said okay. I wanted to tell him the other part. I knew it was a sin to go to his apartment, but now that I had started I had to finish. We took the crowded subway down to Grand Central and walked through, silently, to the Times Square Shuttle. I have never been so afraid in my life. We took the Broadway train up to where he lived. The only thing he could say was he was glad I was being so frank. I didn't say anything.

"He had a nice apartment, neat like his appearance. I was immediately attracted by the softness of everything. The colors were soft and the lights were soft, not low or dim or anything, but soft. There was almost no wood or glass in the living room, yet it wasn't overstuffed.

"My husband was working two jobs, but even at that we

Day of Furious Intent 79

could never afford a place like this. It was in the middle of a ghetto, but it was very nice.

"He offered me a drink. I refused. This was the first time I had been to the apartment of another man since I got married.

"He drank vodka and orange soda. I didn't want him sitting on the same side of the room with me. I asked him to sit in a chair across the room. He was making me nervous. I felt that in back of his gentleness there was a big possibility of violence. I told him I was afraid of him.

"'You think I would hurt you?' he asked.

"'Yes.'

"He paused. 'Do you think I would hit you with my fist or hurt you sexually?' he said, revealing for the first time that he knew all along what the meaning was of the looks he gave me.

"'Both,' I said. I was breathing hard.

"He paused again. 'You think I would hit a woman?'

"'Yes.' I did think he would hit me if he knew what was on my mind. If he found out that I was very attracted to him and knew that he was very attracted to me but that I would never make love to him because he was black.

"'Are you built very small?' He was ready to make his approach to me.

"'What?'

"'Is your thing,' he said pointing between my legs, 'built very small? Is that why you think I would hurt you sexually?'

"'I'm built small,' I said, not knowing why I was telling this man all these personal things about me.

"'I'm a gentle lover. I wouldn't hurt you,' he said. He was sure now that he had me.

"'I'm very attracted to you,' I said. 'But I'm afraid of you because of the things that I have thought about you.'

"'Like what?'

"'That you really want to make love to me and you never will and that I want to make love to you and never will. I could see in your eyes that you wanted me.'

"'Yes. I wanted you.' He stood up.

"I was breathing harder now. I was feeling the hottest sexual flush I had ever felt. I was dizzy. I could feel the heavy softness of my own thighs yielding to him. I could see the budge in his trousers. He was breathing hard.

" 'I could never make love to you,' I said.

" 'Because I am black?'

" 'Yes, you are black,' I said. 'I could never let you make love to me,' I said, 'because you are black.'

" 'I'm black,' he said. 'Do you think I'm dying to make love to you because you're almost white?'

" 'Yes.' I didn't care if he hated me. 'You're a nigger,' I said. I glared at him. I was afraid, but if he tried to hit me I would tear his flesh with my teeth. I would scratch him.

" 'Do you think I've ever made love to a white woman?'

" 'Many times.'

" 'Do you think you're superior to me?'

" 'Yes.'

" 'Are you attracted to me because I'm black?'

" 'Yes.'

" 'Could you ever love a black man?' His questions came at me too fast for me to lie.

" 'No,' I said. 'Never . . . never.' Then I told him I wanted to leave. I was ice-cold. I was afraid that he would kill me.

"He tried to get me to stay by telling me that nothing would happen to me. He said he was enjoying the talk and he admired my honesty and it was doing him good to hear these things.

"I wasn't interested in doing him good. I wanted to get out of there. I picked up my coat and left. This happened on a Friday. That Monday, I didn't go to work. When I went back, on Wednesday, I was afraid. In the morning he said hello, nothing more. Later in the day he whispered, 'The two days you were out can count as sick days. That way, you won't have to lose the vacation time. I can fix it up that way.' That was all he said.

"During the following weeks, my work started to improve and I started enjoying the job for the first time. Later in the

Day of Furious Intent   81

year, I quit. Several times he tried to get in touch with me, but I never responded, but if there is something special about love, then that would be it for me. I was in love with him in this special way. That's the strongest feeling of love I've ever felt.

6

Laying Dead

They say if you're not in love you're only half alive.
That certainly isn't true.

"How do I respond to love? I respond by running from it. I'm not afraid. I just don't like to get backed into a corner. I avoid anything that's extremely intense. On a scale of one to ten, if anything is more intense than a three, don't bring it near me.

"I don't like my emotions to go out of control. I like to be cool and controlled at all times. While my emotions are in control, I can do more things career-wise. Loss of control seems to me a sign of immaturity, so I tend to cool myself out. I'm not like I was when I was eighteen. When I was eighteen I was very much in love, yes, oh, yes. I was very much in love. It was with a guy named César."

The time before when I had talked to her, she was brisk and modern. It was at the end of a work day. I could see in her eyes that she was dead tired. Sweat had made her makeup run and had caused her face to shine. She had been irritable and easily annoyed by personal questions.

Now she was not nearly so pretty and certainly not as irritable. She was at home, in her small apartment without a real kitchen. Curtains covered a cooking alcove along a wall in front of the tiny bathroom. There was not enough closet space, so some of her clothing was stacked in a corner.

No one from out of town would guess that in New York a place like this cost $275 per month. It was on the fifth floor and there was no elevator up. Two windows in the front were sunny, but there were no windows on either side, and only one high, dingy window in the back, in the bathroom, that looked out on a narrow air shaft.

"I met César at a college dance. He asked me to dance and he was acting so silly. He was so silly. After the dance he walked me back to the dormitory and I just started liking him because he was so silly," she said. A dog barking in the hallway made us stop for a moment. She went to the cooking alcove, where water was boiling for tea. She was a tall woman who was not thin but had thin limbs, who was wide-set but fleshless.

"There was a pureness about him, in a way, a kind of innocence in the way he saw things. His impression of things was unclouded, unclouded by other people's opinions." She came back to the front of the room and her voice became less shrill. She could almost whisper now.

"For example, his idea about work. He never worked, because he didn't feel that he had to. He felt that he was being victimized by white society. He felt that society owed him something because he had been victimized.

"He was raised in the slums of East Harlem, and he was very, very bitter. Yet there was something paradoxical about that. His bitterness freed him. You always hear about bitterness hanging people up, bitterness being a prison, but this was just the opposite. His bitterness set him free. He wasn't weighted down with a lot of conventions. He didn't feel that he had to do what other people expected him to do. He felt that if society had shown no responsibility toward him, then he was not obligated to feel any responsibility toward it.

"He was smart enough not to be antisocial; he was asocial. He didn't just go out and commit rebellious crimes, but there was a wild freedom with him which made it possible for him to do anything that did not cost him, personally, too much. If you want me to talk about love I would have to talk about that. I really love César.

"He introduced me to a lot of new things:—to smoking pot. I hate the word *pot*. It sounds so middle class. Let's say he introduced me to the herb. I began to drink, go to discos, to keep late hours. I began to enjoy life for the first time.

"I think one reason was that our backgrounds were so different. I grew up in the suburbs. In Connecticut. It was a black neighborhood, but most of my schooling had been with white kids.

"I felt I had been victimized too, but I felt victimized at a much earlier age, and in a much more passive, subtle way. So I guess what you had was two victims, being free—not so much in what we did. We weren't wild and didn't do anything all that rebellious, but we just lived, everywhere. All up and down New York, in the village by N.Y.U., on the subways, at Coney Island, uptown, walking around midtown, laughing and acting silly. It was great.

"It was great feeling that you don't own the world, so you're free to do anything you want to in it. We just kissed and giggled, kissed and giggled. Bitterness can be very liberating if you've got the right kind of head, especially when you're very young.

"César was different from anything I had seen. Before I met him, I had been going out with a guy who was very, very clean. Very nice. Very well-mannered. The kind of guy your parents want you to marry. He was so clean that he disgusted me. Never said a curse word in front of a girl. Always made sure the girl walked on the inside—you know, when walking on the sidewalk. Always on time for a date. I didn't have time for that shit—then—although he is the kind of guy I would marry right now.

"César was different. He had this *macho* about him. This sense of maleness about him. I was fascinated by that, and it wasn't because there was anything physically very *macho* about him. He was very scrawny. Here I am five foot nine. I must have outweighed him by around ten pounds, but still he could assert himself. I couldn't get over that, this little skinny dude telling me what to do. I'm a very assertive woman and always have been, but there was something about him that was able to make me do what he wanted me to do.

"I look back and I laugh at it now. I was so much in love. I don't look back with regrets, though. I have a good life, I guess. In a few years I'll be one of the four or five best-known black models in the world. I've gotten offers from Rome, Paris, all over. Designers know me. I work too hard to get really lonely; I work hard and come home too tired to worry about love. I like eating in fine restaurants, and then most of the time I come home and go to bed by myself. That's a very satisfying life for me. I have a nice little arrangement with a nice dude who takes care of the sexual part of my life. He's very busy too. He wants to open his own, black-owned stockbrokerage firm in a few years. He will.

"I can't say I'm in love with him. If he had to move to San Francisco tomorrow, I would miss him but I wouldn't follow. It might seem cold to say, but his leaving would be no more than a temporary inconvenience. I'm not saying that it would be easy to find another lover to replace him. He's a very nice guy. We enjoy ourselves together and he's fantastic in bed. César was not that good in bed, but I loved him more. So you see, sex isn't it.

"César was laughable self-confident. It didn't make any sense to judge César, mostly because your judgments wouldn't make any difference to him. Each time he made love to you it was such a ceremony, like he was giving you a gift. He placed such a high value on himself that you automatically felt that he was honoring you when he gave you himself. I have to smile now when I remember him, but it's a warm smile, because I do miss that strange little Puerto Rican. I didn't judge him. He didn't invite comparisons. All I know is I felt very, very complete when we finished the little bit of love-making we did.

"There was something else about César that will tell you something about me. César had a way of making me feel sorry for him. Even though he dominated me, totally, I also felt sorry for him—because he was scrawny. I always had a thing for strays—stray birds, stray cats, stray anything. There's a maternal streak in me that I've managed to hide, but César played on it.

"It was always there. I remember, once when I was about four years old, I was reading this Walt Disney-type story and there was a duck, and a whole gang, a whole host of characters started beating on this duck. I went into hysterics. I kept screaming at these characters to stop beating on the duck. I was screaming and crying. I almost went crazy.

"I don't know why, I've just always had a soft spot for anything that is small and pitiable and victimized. And combine that with César's gorgeous hazel eyes and he could get me to do anything he wanted me to do, yes. I know I was in love because I used to cry so much for him. When he'd go off and I didn't see him for a few days, I would worry about him, and I would start calling around to all of his friends, crying, 'Have you seen César? Have you seen César? Do you know where he could be?'

"I didn't know until later that he used to stay away on purpose just to bruise me. His love magic wouldn't work unless he bruised me and made me worry and fret over him, and he had a way of making me feel guilty. He'd say, 'I hate everything you stand for. I hate your middle-class ways.' This was one of his ways of dominating me. Before that, I had never considered myself middle class. What did I have? My mother was a domestic. My father was a mechanic. True, we had a house, and you might say that any black family that owns a house was middle class.

"So César made me feel guilty in order to get me to do things for him, when really I had been hurt by society too and I needed acceptance from him. I had been in schools with nothing but white kids, and though I wasn't excluded from things—I was even pushed into things by my white teachers and I was put into more things than most of the white kids. The white teachers bent over backwards to make sure I had good parts in the school plays and in the school assemblies. Whenever there was a special program, I was always one of the ones selected. And in high school the counselors worked with me and made sure I got good college scholarships.

"For example, I had a full ride to N.Y.U., where César and I met, so in a way I was middle class. He had come to N.Y.U. on a special program designed especially for disadvantaged kids from New York slum neighborhoods.

"But just being the only black kid in my high school classes had hurt me in very subtle ways and had made me very vulnerable, and so César could use this as a means of pimping off on me. I didn't have much money but I gave him money. He was as smart as I was, but I stayed in the dormitory doing his homework. I ran errands for him. He made a little extra money selling pot and I carried his pot for him and stashed it in my room for him.

"He never gave me reassurance. He would literally drain me with sad stories about how he had been raised by his mother in the jungles of East Harlem. His father was a Cuban merchant marine who had dozens of children by different women. He told me that sometimes he didn't see his father for years—which was true, but I found out later that his mother owned the apartment building where they lived and she had property in Puerto Rico. I found out that his mother had always given him everything he wanted and had spoiled him. He had actually been a more well-to-do kid than I was, dig that!

"So I learned this but, even so, every time I tried to think of myself, I would think about all this religious bullshit that my parents had put into my head as a child. I'd remember from Sunday school how it was better to pity the unfortunate, and to try to raise them up. So it was in part this jive Baptist religion that kept me loving him long after I knew he was lying to me. I couldn't think of myself, because I was always thinking of him and trying to understand his side of everything. I mean, after all, he was a liar, so something had to be wrong with him and I had to feel sympathy for him for that, and I had to try and make him see that lying was not the best way, and that he was only hurting and torturing himself.

"That's the way I was thinking at the time, but the funny thing was that he wasn't hurting or torturing himself. He was hurting and torturing me. Then, in his junior year of college, he got a better scholarship to Marquette University. It was a full ride through the rest of undergraduate school with a full ride through law school. He took it without blinking an eye. He left me without blinking an eye.

"For the first weeks after he was gone, I thought I was going to die. My body ached for him. He said he loved me and that he would come back to New York to see me as often as he could. He said he would write me every day, but I didn't hear from him. I worried that something had happened to him. I called his mother and she told me rather contemptuously that he was all right. I stayed in my room wondering why he didn't write. I thought I was gonna go crazy. I wrote him and he didn't answer my letters. I was constantly on the verge of taking a plane out to Milwaukee to see if there was something I had done wrong.

"Then, one night, he called me from Chicago and we talked for hours. He was telling me how great school was and about how he was planning to stay out there and go into politics when he finished law school and how he was meeting all sorts of people who could help him with his career.

"We talked for hours about everything, and I kept waiting for him to talk about us, about what plans he had for us. I actually would've married him and washed his clothes and had his babies. I loved him that much. But he never mentioned us. Then, finally, I asked him directly about us and he said that he loved me, that he would always love me and that I would be his woman again as soon as he got on his feet. As he went on and on, the things he said began to hurt me more and more, because they sounded so beautiful and they were exactly what I wanted for my life. But they hurt, because I could feel that César was just incapable of meaning any of that. He wasn't lying, exactly, he was just incapable of caring about anyone but himself.

"Then, when he hung up, the operator called back and said the party on the other end wished to reverse charges to my phone and would I accept the charges. I said, 'No.' They threatened to take my phone out, but I knew I would die and go to hell before I let them charge that call to my telephone. And they didn't, either. I wrote letters, I went down to the phone company and I threatened to take them to court. I did everything to make them leave my phone alone, and they did. And finally they stopped threatening me. Meanwhile, I never heard from César again.

7
As Real As Real

Anything in the world, you can find right here in the Bronx.

"I wish I could get a fool to fall in love with me so I could waste him. I'd take every penny he got," Norma said and laughed.

"Rightee-e," Shirley agreed.

"I'd be real nice to him till I got him, then I'd take him for everything. Everything!" Both of the women laughed this time. Norma continued: "I'd probably get him to marry me so he can't wiggle out of it. Then I'd take him to see the judge." She laughed again, but this time Shirley didn't join her.

"Whyn' you be nice to Alfred? If you'd be nice to him, you could get anything you want. We'd be on easy street." It is obvious the two of them had argued this point before.

Norma claimed that Alfred was not as big a fool as Shirley thought. She didn't like being blamed for letting a good fish get off the matrimonial hook. "His wife got all his money, anyway," she said. "All he keeps is a little chump change." In the dim light of the room, Norma's face seemed attractive. It was well made up and perhaps it really was pretty beneath the inch-long eyelashes that cast long shadows on dark cheeks, tinted maroon with facial magic. Her lips were red. The trim, upper part of her body sat on a pair of the biggest thighs that ever squeezed out of a twenty-six-inch waist. "Black men ain't shit," she said.

"Rightee-e," Shirley agreed.

"Why do you say that?" I asked

"Because they ain't," she said. "What you got to do is build a man up, build him up and build him up till he thinks he's hot shit, and then you lower the boom." They laughed. They hugged each other and leaned together and laughed. I wonder how many other women thought as she thought. I bet that most of those who did were not willing to admit it, even to themselves.

"Alfred is married, and all he wants is a little young tail. He ought to go home to his wife, the old dog. That's what I call him to his face, a old yellow dog," Norma said. Her giant thighs threatened to burst out of her skirt as she wiggled on the sofa.

"See," Shirley said.

Norma paid her no mind. "I don't think it's wrong to take his money and not be in love with him. He got plenty. If he want to give it to you, go ahead and take it. Take it!" They scream and lean together, laughing. "Take it!" said these young girls, hot as firecrackers. Norma is only twenty. Shirley is twenty-one.

"He lives over in Jersey in a fine home, honey. His wife was away last summer, so he took a bunch of us over there. Showing off."

"Yeah, showing off," Shirley said. "I tried to eat everything he had in his refrigerator."

"He got the fireplace and the wall-to-wall carpet, and club basement—showing us all these things he had. So when he came by here the next time I made him buy me a full-length rabbit coat," she said. She wears the rabbit coat like a mink, all over the Bronx. Her tiny head glides above it. Her giant hips wiggle under it. The hugh thighs roll around each other. They are so big that only by rolling can she put one foot in front of another. Hers is a strange walk which makes men say, "Good God Almighty," when she passes down the aisle of the Pathmark, shopping for groceries.

"He don't mess with ladies who got as much as he got. He only messes with women in the lower-development-type apartments or projects or who might be on welfare or something. This makes him feel big with his old self. So any woman who can take some of the old fool's money, more power to her. I'm gonna get mine or he's gonna get none of this." She patted herself on the thighs.

The game, the way she ran it, was a lot cruder than I had seen it run, but in this raw form at least it exposed itself for what it honestly was. It was an exchange. He was trading money for youth and beauty; she was a beauty. She obviously took a lot of time to make herself up. She looked very clean. Her eyelashes were on straight. No doubt she had taken a cosmetology course somewhere. Her clothing was well co-ordinated: black and white polka-dot Quiana blouse with loose-fitted turtle neckline that hung low enough to expose the soft reddish-black skin where her collarbones were invisible under the padding of flesh; black skirt, stylishly short.

No doubt Alfred got his money's worth: big, soft, clean with a beautiful reddish glow to her skin. She was not a prostitute. She was a courtesan, though the term is seldom used on people of her economic status. She was a mistress.

Alfred dropped by her place four or five times a week. He owned several apartment buildings in the Bronx. He owned a laundromat and he owned the building where Norma lived, where I interviewed Norma and Shirley. In exchange for loving him, Norma did not have to pay rent. He didn't mind.

He was a cynical little bright-skinned man who claimed he had a better deal with Norma than he had with his wife. At least he was getting something from Norma in return for his money. From his wife he was getting nothing, and her spread cost four times as much as Norma's did. I had talked to him in his laundromat, down near Tremont.

Though he lived in New Jersey, he stayed in the Bronx all day enjoying himself. He did have a nice deal. He got home-cooked food when he wanted it, and was never without someone to talk to. He liked his life. He liked the Bronx, where he had been raised, much more than Jersey, where his wife had forced him to move. He believed in love. He said he loved Norma. He said if she ever needed help, he would be there. When she went into the hospital, he came to see her. Out in Jersey, sometimes he dreamed about her. If he ever got a divorce, he would ask her to marry him.

He dresses in run-down suits instead of easier-to-keep casual clothes. By midday he is rumpled, sitting in the laundromat watching his machines, and giving out change. "Sure," he says. He knows a whole lot about love. "Norma knows I do," he says and laughs. I am talking to him two days after I talked to Norma and Shirley for the first time. He is a talkative little man.

"He talks too much," Norma had said. In the dingy afternoon I watched him talk. His little mustache rides his small, pinched lip.

"He comes past here," Norma had said, "with a lot of garbage. I let him talk. I go on and do what I got to do and let him talk. He's such a fool." She had said up in the apartment that she was getting free from him. "I can't stand no man who let anyone make a fool out of them, even if the person is me who's making the fool out of them. I can't stand him," she had said. "A man got to be a man. He's got to be in control of his thing."

Economically, Alfred is very well in control of his thing. He dispenses change of a dollar to a fat girl with corn-row braids. The braids are coming loose, giving her sprays of black, straw-like hair all over her head. Alfred comes back to sit down. "Sure I believe in love. You got to believe in it in some form," he says.

"I don't like a man who lets people run over him," Norma had said.

Shirley had cut in: "You can stay with someone for the money, but you can't love that person if you think that person's a fool. You can stay with a person because that person's real nice to you, but that's not really love. I got to feel like you're a real man before I can love you."

"What's a real man?" I had asked.

"I can't describe it," Shirley had said. She had gotten out into deep water; her vocabulary was too small to express the complexity of her feelings. She had called on Norma for help. "You know what I mean, Norma?" It had been a timid question, which showed that Shirley was aware of her limitations as far as explaining herself went, and these limitations may have been the reason for her shyness, the reason why she was Norma's side-kick, instead of vice versa, for in her way Shirley was more appealing to a higher class of men than Norma. She was trimmer, yet very well built, with beautiful smooth, dark legs.

Her face was square. It had more character, but, lacking confidence, she didn't try to sell what she had. She didn't package herself well. Norma's clothes were the kind you had to send to the cleaners to get blocked. Shirley's flowered dress could be washed and worn without ironing.

"Rick was what you would call a man," Norma had said, not

so much coming to Shirley's rescue as taking back the spot-light.

"Yeah, Ricky was what you would call a real man." Shirley's voice had trailed off.

"I loved Ricky. Shirley'll tell you. I really loved Ricky. I was young and dumb. Anyone who gets that much in love has to be young and dumb." Her face was suddenly sad. The tension that kept her jaws tight had left, and her face had seemed fat and slack. She was sadly fat for the first time. Before, she had been a big, round good-time girl—the kind you could see dancing in a bright red dress with the dress riding her hinnie in the back, and clinging as if wet to her mammoth thighs in front. She had seemed younger.

I had pictured what she would look like without her wig, without her girdle holding her stomach from sagging like a sack of woe down into her lap. She'd look like a young girl, which she is, and an old woman, too.

Alfred says that he loves both images of her, the images he sees, the glamour girl and the child. He makes love to one while he holds a fantasy picture in mind of the other. "It's just a nitty-gritty feel about the Bronx," he says. "They got some slums up here and then they got some nice places. Just over in Riverdale they got some of the most expensive real estate in New York. I don't need to leave the Bronx and I can get whatever I want." His face is animated in the filter light that comes through the grimy windows of his laundromat. An old yellow dog, that's what Norma said she called him.

Five red lights glow on the front of his dryers. Each light represents another dime for him. Through the glass doors of ten of his washers, I see suds sloshing around, or rinse water coming down across brightly colored clothing. Each washer is grossing fifty cents for him. His apartments, most of them sitting idle with adult tenants off at work earning rent money and kids off at school, each apartment just sitting there making money for him. He is a capitalist.

"There's no love between me and my wife," he says. "With the kids grown, we just stay together for presentation sake."

"Does she have a man friend?"

"Yes. We go our own way, do our own thing." I watch him and see that he didn't like that question, but he doesn't stay worried for long. He is a man used to sorting out and casting out. The thought of her male friend is absolutely no use to him. He casts it out.

"I been with Norma since she was nineteen. I got a daughter older than her. My daughter goes to Michigan State. She gon' graduate at the end of the summer. I'll drive out there," he says.

I think about his gray Cadillac, parked outside. I think about the hundreds of miles between here and Michigan, he and his wife riding without saying more than a few dozen words to each other: "At the next rest stop I have to go to the bathroom," she might say. Nothing much more.

Successful men make willing truces with life. These truces are how a society is held together. So much of what is emotional must take place below the surface. "That's why the Gay Liberation people are selfish and shortsighted," a psychologist friend had said some months before. "If all the closet doors, all of them in all forms, were opened, we would have chaos." I had accused him of talking like a sociologist. He had reminded me that that's what he had gone to college to be until he changed his focus to the problems of the individual rather than the problems of the mass.

He believed that, in order to exist, all of us must have our little secrets, no matter how dirty, but we must never be so selfish as to want to expose these secrets on a mass scale.

"Hey," Alfred yells suddenly, "stop kicking that goddam machine, boy." An adolescent boy in red-striped shirt had started kicking a soap-dispensing machine that had cheated him out of his coin. Alfred walks down and opens the machine, using one of the keys that he has attached to a ring on his belt loop. The keys are part of the reason that his suits are pulled out of shape. He gives the pouting boy his coins, then he walks back and sits again beside me on the park-style bench that runs down the center of the dingy, linoleum-covered floor.

"Little niggers don't know how to take care of nothing," he

says loud enough for the boy to hear. "For one lousy dime he's gonna tear the damn machine apart. That's why I don't fix this place up. What's the use?" He doesn't stay angry long. "Yeah, man, there's a lot of fun left in these old bones."

"How old?"

"Fifty-six. I been married twenty-nine years this September," he says.

"Twenty-nine."

"That's right. It used to be rough. I used to get upset, but that's what you got to learn about life in order to be successful: Don't fight what you can't change. Don't get into scraps you can't win. Trying to change another person is something you can't do. See, just like you've got things in your personality that you can't or don't want to change, other people have too, even if they are bad things, even if you know they're bad. That's the biggest thing I've learned in life. It does no good to point out to people some bad feature of their lives. They won't change. They'll only resent you and find something equally bad to point out about your personality."

He gets up and gives change to a plump woman in a jean skirt. He is already talking when he sits down again. "And the other thing I learned is that you don't get something for nothing. If someone gives you something and tells you it's free, watch out." He leaned close and laughed. "I put a little money in Norma's pockets," he says, "she don't pay rent. That gives me freedom to come and go as I please," he whispers.

"Then, maybe she doesn't love you. Maybe she loves your money."

He smiles. "Loving my money, that's loving me. She can't get the money without loving me. I'm no fool." He leans close and whispers more softly, "See?"

"But wouldn't it be nice to know that she loves you for more reasons than that?"

"Oh, she does, I have no doubts of that," he says, still leaning close, touching me with a finger and by this contact drawing me into his conspiracy. "It couldn't be only that."

"But her love is too closely tied to her self-interest, to her financial interest."

"I don't know 100 per cent that that's true. I do know she is very fond of me," he says, still leaning close. I listen to hear if he has even a bit of doubt in his voice, to see if there is a slight hint that he is asking for confirmation from me that she is fond of him. No self-doubt creeps in. He continues. "I represent something to her. It could be a father image, it could be success, I don't know."

"But would she love you if you didn't have the money," I ask, looking up directly into his eyes, feeling that I had him in a trap.

"That's a stupid question, in a way," he says. "I do have the money and she does love me. If I didn't have the money I would have to deal with that. But, for that matter, I don't think anyone would love me that much without money. For example, my own daughter. My daughter calls me two or three times a month from Michigan. Each time she calls, I tell her that I saw something pretty that I'm going to send her; or else she asks me for something she needs. If I didn't have it to give, she wouldn't call. She would call, oh, yeah. She would call on Christmas and my birthday, maybe, if I'm lucky, if she happens to remember. She would call because society requires that she call on Father's Day, but there wouldn't be that same warmth. She would just call and say, 'Happy Father's Day, Dad. How's Momma? How are you?' a few meaningless things like that, or she would send me a Father's Day card with words on it that she had never read. But now when she calls we talk. We have a good time. She thinks I'm a great old guy. She tells her friends that her daddy is a swinger. She loves me. Is she faking? No. . . . You see what I mean?" This is the first time he has asked for confirmation. "Nobody wants you when you're down and out, isn't that what the song says?"

"That's a hard view on human nature," I say.

"I'm a realist, son."

"But wouldn't it be nice to know that someone would love you even if you had nothing?"

"No," he says flatly, so flatly that the words sit out like a physical thing in the air of the laundromat. I see some of the toughness in him that I saw when he handled the boy who was kicking the soap machine. "I wouldn't want to be loved under those conditions, because that would not be love. That would be pity, man, and I would rather someone hate me than feel sorry for me." He laughs, certain that he is right.

Shirley lives in Norma's apartment off and on; sometimes she lives at home with her parents. She entertains company at Norma's, so it is her love nest too. "Norma was crazy about Ricky, this boy named Ricky," Shirley said. She got up from the sofa and went to put a record on the stereo, a forty-five that took a long time to drop down and start to play. Then she put a stack of records on the spindle and placed the automatic changer arm over the stack. "That's what I said," Norma added. "If you want to talk about pure love. There is a difference." She adjusted her weight on the plastic slip covers that protected the imitation tiger-skin upholstery of her sofa.

The place was so neat that it looked almost unlived in. The formica tops of the tables were spotless. The pea-green walls seemed untouched, and the two framed dime-store pictures of bongo players were perfectly centered above the sofa. A silver chain ran up between the pictures and across a portion of the ceiling and then hung down to support a bird-cage lamp.

"Shirley'll tell you how much I loved Ricky. I was bad off, child." She leaned a little sideways and covered her mouth as people do when they are about to cough. She didn't cough, but laughed. This is a gesture I had seen before, this habit of hiding laughter behind the hand. "Shoot, you have more fun when you don't have some nigger always hanging around you, like last summer me and Shirley and this other girl went to California.

"It was great. We went out with these three fellows and we drained them niggers. We were all down at the Brown Derby. You know we didn't have no business at no Brown Derby or some such expensive place as that. We made them take us to the Ginza. That's why I say men are stupid. We had to pay three dollars apiece at the door, and if you wanted to go downstairs to dance you had to pay eight dollars for a table downstairs. It was ridiculous. So Shirley said we didn't need a table downstairs, she was trying to save the fellows some money, but I said I wanted to sit down, shoot. If they gon do it, then let them do it.

"That why I say you should never let nobody waste your money, but if fools let you do it, go ahead and do it. They wanted to show off and so they got the table downstairs. That's why I say men are suckers. I can understand if a man makes $50,000 or $100,000 a year—I can understand him spending $150 or $200 or $250 to take some chicks out—but these suckers lived in the projects. They didn't have that much money, but here was these three fine chicks from New York, so they had to show out—Don't ever let anybody make a fool out of you.

"This guy made me so sick, when we got back to his apartment I didn't even kiss him. I don't want things to come to me on a silver platter. I want to see what it is to struggle to get what I want. If I marry a millionaire, that's different. He's supposed to give to me, but if you're just an ordinary person you can't be giving your money away.

"But men do that. My girl friend got this man fifty years old, and he's a fool. He ain't getting nothing from her, but every week he takes her down to Pathmark and buys her ten or fifteen bags of groceries. She just go along the shelves picking things out, whether she wants them or not. Ain't he stupid?

"If I was going to get married I would rather hook a fool than worry about someone I was in love with. Love makes you be a fool and you come out worst off.

"I remember, when I was twelve and thirteen, I used to have a lot of crushes, you might say, for older men, like in junior high school my music teacher. I couldn't even go to music classes, because I didn't want to see that man. When I saw him, Mr. Johnson, Mr. Tyrone Johnson, I mean I just couldn't set up in class and look at him. It made me feel like I wanted to pee on myself whenever he called on me. You remember Mr. Johnson, Shirley?"

Shirley shook her head, no. She was up dancing to Archie

Bell and the Drells singing "Tighten-up." The playing of the music seemed to be Shirley's act of independence, rebellion.

"Shirley, you did know Mr. Johnson."

"I didn't know him. I don't remember all those people."

"You're so dumb," Norma said.

Shirley continued her funny little ditty of a dance. Subtle rhythms worked through her; she didn't have to move much to stay inside the music. The hem of her yellow dress swished playfully about her legs. Her hips had set the dress in motion, so it was moving two beats to each beat of Shirley's legs. "Ah-h-h," she said and rolled her eyes at her friend.

In disgust Norma sucked at the roof of her mouth. "Anyway, I couldn't go to music, so at the end of the year he gave me a "F," so you see what love'll do for you. I got a flat "F," you hear me? and my Momma beat my ass good.

"Then, when I was in eighth grade, I had very strong feelings for this man who was about forty years old. It was the lady I used to stay with, her brother. I used to stay with her until my mother came home from work. My father had croaked when I was eleven, and my mother used to work funny hours, so I used to stay with this woman, Mrs. Hodges. It was her brother. We used to call him Uncle Billy. I fell in love with that man.

"He just struck me as a fine-looking man, because in the eighth grade I wasn't looking for someone to do anything for me. I wasn't thinking about him buying me things or anything like that. It was just pure feeling based on the fact that he was so damn fine. Shirley, Shirle-e-e-e!"

Shirley came up out of the music and looked at us.

"Shirley, you remember Uncle Billy. Wasn't he fine?"

"And you loved that Negro," Shirley answered.

"See? That's how love always gets you in trouble. That's what I was saying. One time, they was having this party and my mother had come home early from work. And they was all around in Mrs. Hodges' house drinking beer and sweating and swearing, so I decided to take a ride with Uncle Billy, and when I got back to Mrs. Hodges' house, my mother was there:

As Real As Real 105

'Where you been with this old man?' Bam! She went up side my head.

"I hadn't been anywhere or done anything bad. It was just a case of pure feeling. That's what love is, this pure feeling. But every time I got the pure feeling, you know how it fills you up and you swell up inside?" She used her hands to show how love rises in you and expands. Her face was wracked with one of those expressions that can be read as a sign of pain or a sign of ecstasy. "Every time in my life when I had this pure feeling something bad happened. . . .

"I was crazy about Uncle Billy, but I wasn't doing anything with him except passing a few kisses and stuff. I was a virgin at the time. I was a virgin up to the time I fell in love with this other boy. That was my first full love affair. I was fourteen. He was eighteen. That was the first time I made love to a man. He got all in my cakes over in Mount Morris Park one night. Shirley was there. We were all there having a good time, and he took me a little ways off and, Oh, my God.

"But shortly after that he went into the Army, and he only came home every couple months or so, but looks like this made the love stronger. This was this boy named Ricky. You remember I told you about this boy I loved when I was a young dumb fool. I loved that nigger.

"All day long in school I used to pretend I was his wife and I was waiting for him to come home from the Army, and he would be wounded and I would have to take care of him all my life. When I was home cooking, I used to pretend that I was cooking for him. I had it bad, and at night I dreamed that I was having his baby. In fact every time he came home and we made love and he went back I used to think I was pregnant. I used to hope I was pregnant, because we wasn't using any kind of protection.

"I tried to stay in love with him, but this guy Herman got on my case. Following me everywhere, talking to me, telling me what he could do to me if he got his hands on me. Herman was a lot of fun to be around. Shirley, you remember Herman Williams?"

106   *Love, Black Love*

Shirley was now in the kitchen. "Herman Williams, yeah, I remember that fool."

"I never was in love with Herman, but he was just a nice person to be around and he let you have your freedom. He wasn't always jealous."

"Right-e-e-e," Shirley said and returned to the room. She smoothed the back of her yellow dress out under her before she sat down on the plastic slip covers.

"Herman loved basketball," Norma said. "He was a basketball nut. He used to live on the playground. He was stupid. If he was wearing a new leather suit and he saw a basketball game he would get in the game and come home three hours later with his suit all messed up. He was stupid. He played basketball in new Stacy Adams shoes. He didn't care.

I moved in with him because my mother was getting on my nerves and Herman was very easy to live with. Whatever you said to him he would agree, as long as you didn't mess with his basketball. Shirley was almost living there too."

"Rightee-e," Shirley said. "Yeah, I used to be over there all the time. Herman was really nice. He would give you the world. If I had a boy friend and I wanted to be with him, Herman would take money out of his own pocket and buy something nice to drink. He was very nice, Norma."

"He was," Norma agreed. "That's why I say a strong like for a person is better than love. He would give me anything I wanted, but he wouldn't let me make a fool out of him. That was the difference. I'd say, 'Herman, give me twenty dollars,' and he would give it to me if he had it, but I could never make a fool of him, or get sassy in his face or curse him out. I don't think he would hit a woman, but he just carried himself in a way that made you respect him. So it got very nice after a while.

"I mean, I would know, when he didn't come home from work, that he had stopped at the playground to play ball, so I would just automatically take his sneakers and old clothes down there, so he wouldn't mess up his good stuff. He would change right on the playground and I would bring his good stuff back home. He was like a little kid in a way. He was never the kind of person who would get on your nerves."

"Norma, I think you was in love with Herman," Shirley said, looking down to make sure the tape recorder heard her.

"But it wasn't like the feeling I had for Ricky. But I think I would have married Herman if he hadn't croaked. I was in the mood to get married. He didn't mind getting married. Married or not, it didn't make no difference to him, but then when he knew he had cancer he wanted to get married quick. He had cancer in the bones. I know you can't catch cancer, but after I found out he had it I didn't want to be around him. Every time he touched me I thought about cancer. So I moved back in with my mother. I was feeling bad most of the time. I was feeling bad because he kept calling my mother's house, wanting to see me. I couldn't even answer the phone when I was home alone, because I was afraid it was going to be him begging me to come by.

"When my mother answered the phone she would tell him I wasn't home. I don't know if he's dead yet or not, but he stopped calling. This was the period I went on drugs. I started messing with the nigger upstairs, who was on drugs. I started staying up at his place during the day to get away from the phone ringing, and that's when I started messing with drugs.

I wasn't a junkie. I got better sense than that. I stopped using drugs completely this summer. I'm going to California next summer. I'm tired of New York, anyway.

"If I could get married in California I would get married. I wouldn't have to love the person—just have a strong like. I don't think that most people are in love nowadays. The way divorces and things are going, no. I think if you're in love you wouldn't break up over the slightest little thing, but if someone did the wrong thing to me, I would leave, which proves that I must not be in love with that person in the first place. Love should hold you together, but not like it is in the movies. That's a bunch of phony shit.

"But I like love pictures. I cry when a good love picture

comes on. It's very sad, even though you know all the time that it's not real.

"When you watch the soap operas during the day, that's more like real life: People fucking over each other. This person having a baby by this person's husband. The only thing is they got more money. That's why I bring it all back to money, girl. If I could get hold to a man with the right money, I would marry him in a minute," she said. "And I'd be a good wife to him. Shoot!" She pouted.

"Me too," Shirley said.

8

Heart of Darkness

Of course I hadn't been, because if I were I would still be there.

"I think there's something very attractive about this very cold black man," Sonja said. She is tall and olive-colored. She was born of Jewish parents but has adopted an Arab name for herself and the son she had by one such cold black man with an Arab name. "If he's bitter he has a right to be," she said. "So many times he's surrounded by a shell and you have a tendency to want to get inside that shell. At least I do," she said.

"That's what I feel about the music. I've hung out in jazz clubs since I was eighteen, or actually before that because I had a fake I.D. in high school, so I could get into Slug's and The Half-Note. Maybe that icy shit attracted me. The music is very hot, but having to live the life has made these men very cold, and me being romantic, I guess I wanted to get inside of that."

Sonja and I were sitting in a jazz club. It was early in the evening, before the band was due in. "My son, Sharif, his father was a musician. He's famous. He's doing well now. So I won't mention his name. I think you might know him," she said.

"Don't worry, I do know him," I said. I made a motion to indicate the instrument he played.

She laughed. "He wasn't that famous when I met him. We were poor together. It was great. We lived together for two years; then I woke up one morning and told him I had to get away. I don't know why. I just had to get away from him. I just said, 'I'm leaving.'

"He turned over in bed and said, 'Okay, the sooner the better,' and he began throwing my shit out the window." She laughed. We interrupted our conversation every so often to watch whoever came into the club. Nearly everyone in the place knew her. It was one of the places where black semicelebrities come to eat soul food, listen to good music, and find white girls to give them the admiration or the kind of attention that even superstars do not get in Harlem.

"Do you know why you left him, though?" I asked.

"Yes, it was a lot of things. For one thing, I quit him because after the baby was born I found out he had children by other women. I was the fourth woman he had had children by. And for another thing, I was never very important in his life. I was third in importance. His music came first, and second came reefer, and I came after the reefer." She laughed again, pushing her long hair back over her shoulder. "And he had lied so much. He had a wife and three children in Philadelphia. I didn't know that.

"I don't have any regrets about having the baby by him. I wanted a baby, and the baby's father was a very beautiful person to have a baby by," she said and pulled out a picture of a handsome mulatto boy with fluffy brown curls.

"I got involved with the music first. I used to hang out in Slug's nearly every night during 1966–67. I used to like to watch the musicians putting their entire lives into something they believed in. And after I got involved with the musicians, I began to see how these men were constantly being abused and put down physically, spiritually, and sexually. In order to get a record date you sometimes have to have your masculinity challenged by these record producers, these big guys who are homosexuals. They can have all the chicks they want, because chicks are free now. They don't even have to pay a girl. Millions of girls would love to go to bed with the president of a big record company.

"But these big guys are into breaking men now. Sharif's father, let's call him Alim, since we can't use his real name, well, Alim and I went to lunch once with this very important man who wanted to produce a record for Alim. The man was a roaring queen. He was making passes and sexual innuendoes right in front of my face. He wasn't after me. He was after Alim.

"I had some money at the time and two credit cards, so I told Alim that we didn't have to deal with this man. I was doing some free-lance editing on a feminist newsletter, so I had a little money coming in. That man was such a dead spirit himself that he had to suck the life out of somebody in order to survive. Masculinity is such a freaky thing nowadays. American men are so sexually uninspiring, so tied to their work that they are almost eunuchs.

"They stay in school until they're twenty-five or so. They're kept as babies until they get married," she said. We watch the people coming into the club. "So we have a country being run by all these emotional babies.

"You can look at the face of a man and see the kind of struggle he's had. If he's been in the street since he was fourteen hustling for himself, there's a certain intensity there that I like in a man. Being a romantic, I'm attracted to that.

"I couldn't settle for a man who didn't inspire me. I could be with him simply for the security angle, or just because the person is a nice guy. I could be friends with a person who was a nice guy," she said, "but I couldn't get involved unless that thrill was there. That's what love is to me." She pushed aside her hair again.

"I don't want to be trite; of course, everyone who finishes college is not like this, but growing up is an important struggle, and too many American men have used college to pad them from this struggle. They've been in college for so long that all they know is stinky-finger and beer parties. They're not really men. I think it's terrible to grow old without ever having been through manhood.

"Like, a young man fresh out of college goes to a big brokerage firm, and he thinks he's got a good, secure job until he finds that the chairman of the board is after his ass. So what does he do? I think the choice that too many of the baby college graduates make is to let him have it. There's nothing wrong with this per se, but psychologically few men can deal with having another man fuck him in the ass. They feel completely shattered. Then they go off to some freaky little psychiatrist who tells them that they've been latent homosexuals all their lives anyway, so they accept it to some degree and when they get to be president of a company, they put another generation of bright little wunderkinds through the same thing."

I listened to her, but half my mind was doing something else. I had no way of knowing if she was correct about the homosexual matter in big companies, but I knew from experience that to get to the top in a big company you almost always had to give up a little piece, actually or symbolically, with each step you made up the corporate ladder. That was almost always the price. And they make you pay, with your ass, or your balls, one way or another.

"It's very sad," she said and sipped from her water glass. She put the glass back on the table and ran her finger slowly around the rim as she continued. "I'm not saying I couldn't be attracted to a man who's had a homosexual, or several homosexual, experiences, but I do like a certain toughness in a man. What makes a human being interesting is the struggle he's had, and when you pad yourself from that struggle you end up with a softness and a shallowness that is very uninspiring," she said. I called the waitress and paid the check. The band was about to come on and she was willing to talk if I needed to know more about what she felt about love.

We left the club. As we walked, I thought about some of the reasons that white women defy social customs and mix with black men. During the course of the book, I had heard a lot of these reasons. Some white women are thrown into contact with black people for one reason or another and simply fall in love with a man who happens to be black. Others are not physically attractive and find that getting a desirable black man is easier than getting a desirable white one. Sonja was not in this category. Her crow-black hair was attractive against her olive skin. She was pretty.

I interviewed one very pretty white girl who felt sorry for black people and thought of her pretty whiteness as a gift to be spread among them. A surprising number of women I talked to were in open rebellion against their fathers. They made love to black men with images of their fathers watching.

Some came across the line to see if there is any truth to the sexual rumors about black men, but I had heard black women say that the sexual reputation of black men is undeserved. Others say that it is deserved, and more. A young black man told me that he fucks white women better than he does black women. "Because of all that hate pent up inside me, I give every white woman I get, I give her a super fuck, a vicious fuck, a punishing fuck," he said. The result is that she isn't punished. On the contrary, she enjoys it. So here, as in so many other areas of life, she gets the long end of the stick.

But only about half the time do the relationships have primarily to do with sex. Sometimes they have more to do with other, special kinds of longings. Sonja says that she loves the life-style and therefore can love only men who are associated with it.

Reasons mix and become sometimes timid, sometimes bold motivation. "And, true," Sonja said, "I like the way black men look, some of them, the intense look, so intact, so in touch with themselves and the source of their energy, with the angry face and the leather midicoat trailing in the wind. There's something very attractive about that image."

We walked for a while. "I'm not a promiscuous person, so sex per se is not it. I have a sister, a real Republican, who would jump into bed quicker than I would. She's what they call a swinging single. She belongs to this club. They swap boy friends and stuff. She's been to orgies. I never have. I don't think people associated with jazz are as promiscuous as the swinging singles, from what I've seen."

As we walked, the streets of the Lower East Side were full of Spanish-speaking people. "It's sexual in that I've never been to bed with a man I didn't at first admire, and I admire many of the things that black people happen to be into right now.

"I'm still very much a romantic. I've been in love a dozen times and I've never lost that tingle of first love. I think this is because I have this really fantastic fantasy life. If he's into music or into something political, I can fantasize about it, and that's how I fall in love. Love starts from a fantasy.

"There was this guy— I won't call his name, because I'm sure you know him, too. Even before I knew him I could fantasize a whole life with him, and I wrote it down, how I could fit very romantically with his political struggle that would end in my death, but I would die so beautifully," she laughed. We sat on the stoop to her building.

"He was involved in something very explosive, and the courts were about to decide in his case, and I had this really fantastic dream: What if he has to go underground? Get

Heart of Darkness 117

away, oh wow! I thought about hiding with him and sneaking out to get food, the whole thing.

"That's like being in love. Just watching someone doing something admirable," she said. "I didn't know him then. I had only seen him once or twice, but I could picture him standing up against the courts, the police, the FBI—they were all after him. My fantasy was being a part of that.

"I was dying to meet him. I called it love. It's not the same feeling that I have when I've been intimate with someone, but it's not a bad substitute. That's why when I'm a dirty old woman lusting after young men's bodies I'll always have these romantic feelings equal to love.

"Later I met this person. A friend introduced us. I was sitting at that same table we were sitting at tonight. He was perfect for me, but how could I be perfect for him when my head was in the clouds? For one thing, I was this little Jewish girl—that was his diminutive term for me—and he was this big political celebrity.

"He used to come here and stay all night. We used to look out the window at the FBI agents who were following him. I didn't see him that often. Maybe once or twice a month, when he was away from his other people. Our little affair went on for almost a year before it ended. I ended it one night when he came over and I had this center-fold nude of Henry Kissinger from *The National Lampoon*, and he told me he didn't really believe that that was Henry Kissinger's body.

" 'Sure it is,' I said.

" 'How do you know?' he asked me.

" 'I know because I was once Henry Kissinger's mistress,' I said.

"He said, 'Come on.'

"I said, 'Sure, I used to be his mistress and that's his real body.' Then, for the first time, he approved of me as being someone important enough to be associated with. Because he thought I had been Henry Kissinger's mistress, which of course I hadn't because if I had I would have been his wife: I would have stuck in there to see what that was all about," she said and laughed.

After a while we got up and went into the apartment to

118   *Love, Black Love*

drink her last bottle of wine. The place was small and cluttered. There was only one small room and a small kitchen. The bathroom had no door, only a curtain across the doorway. There was a sleeping alcove curtained off on the other side of the room. Her child was asleep behind the curtain. She wanted me to look in to see. The child was handsome. In the dim light I could see a teen-aged Puerto Rican girl sleeping against a pillow against the wall. She must have been the baby sitter.

So as not to awaken anyone, we took the wine across the hall to the apartment of a girl friend who had been in Morocco for two months.

Her girl friend's apartment was about the same size, but more of the available space was taken up by wall bookcases. Sonja put the Randy Weston *Blue Moses* album on the stereo.

"You dig Weston?" she asked.

"Yeah."

She opened the wine. We sat on the mattress on the floor. "I'm thinking about going to Morocco as soon as I get some of my debts paid. I have to pay off one thousand dollars to American Express that I borrowed for one of *your* brothers."

I laughed.

"I might want to raise my son in North Africa or Europe. I can't decide over here how to raise him. I could raise him as white in a typically Jewish way. I looked at him the other day and caught myself thinking: my son the doctor.

"I have the option. I could give him a very hard-core materialistic upbringing. Like the myth white as opposed to black —black being physical and emotional and white being abstract and calculating and successful because of that. But I guess that's not true any more. A lot of black cats are out there hustling and making very calculated moves. . . ."

I smiled in the dark, thinking to what extent this had always been true.

"My girl friend likes North Africa. I might go there and check that out," she said, "because no matter how much I'd want to, I could never raise him to be the kind of man I admire. I'm too much of a Jewish mother to let him out there on his own in those killing streets."

9

The Mind Blower

I keep looking for someone else and seeing only me.

Though his real name was Clarence Stafford, he called himself The Mind Blower. He cocked his head sideways when he said it, and waited for the impact to register. He smiled; then, when he felt it had soaked in, he grabbed me and yelled, "Aa-a-y-y-y-ya-a."

He had been calling every day for a week, saying, "Hey, when we gon do that interview? How can you do a book on love without talking to The Mind Blower?"

I had already talked to his lady friend. She agreed that he was "a mind blower." She said he was the best man she had ever had. I had been referred to him originally by his ex-wife. She said he was sick. I had met him a few times in midtown Manhattan, but we had not had time to talk. That's when I learned he was calling himself The Mind Blower and when I had seen him cock his head to the side and wait and then grab me and yell.

"Hey, when we gon talk?" he said on the telephone.

"Today; how about today?" I said.

"Okay, I got the perfect setup. We can talk at my lady's place," he said. "She's working late. Why don't we have dinner first at this sidewalk place? We can sit out and watch the ladies. I think it's good, man. This is a nice day for it. I feel good. I feel like giving my analysis of love. Love is a very complicated matter," he said.

"Don't tell me now. Wait," I said. We talked for a while about other things before we hung up. When we sat down to eat, he could barely eat for talking.

"I'm in love. I'm really in love. For the first time in my life, I really love somebody," he said to start.

"That's good. How long have you been in love?"

"About a year. But the love has grown, man. It's heavier now that it once was, and it makes me feel very good."

"You're lucky."

"But you haven't asked me why I'm so much in love."

"No, I haven't. Why are you so much in love?"

"You don't know the answer to that one because you haven't asked me who I'm in love with."

"Okay, who're you in love with?"

He cocked his head to the side and waited. "I'm in love with me," he said.

I wanted to laugh but didn't.

"The only person I love is me," he said. "You said you were writing a book on love, right, well I'm in love. I'm in love with me." He held his head to the side and watched me. "Shocked you, didn't I? You can't dig that, can you?"

"I can dig it. I've been interviewing people for almost a year. By now I've heard just about everything."

"But can you dig that?" he insisted as if he was insisting that I not dig it so easily. He wanted it to have shock value. "I'm having this fabulous love affair with myself. If I had to get married right now, the only person I could possibly marry is me." He stopped and watched me with his head cocked to the side. "That's why I call myself The Mind Blower."

The waiter gave me back my credit card and we left the restaurant. "You're having a love affair with yourself," I repeated as we headed down Fourth Street.

"It blows people's minds when I tell them that. They expect me to at least laugh and make a joke of it, but I'm serious."

"Serious."

"Serious as a heart attack. Is cancer serious?"

"You know, in reality a lot of people are in love with themselves," I said. "You're not really that unique."

"Yeah, but I don't mean it that way. I mean, I'm having a love affair with myself. I have a girl friend, but you'll notice I'll say I like her very much but I'll never say I love her. I need her. I feed on her in so many ways and she feeds on me. It's a symbiotic relationship, but it's not love." The street was crowded and he had to stop talking every so often when we were separated by people passing between us or when either he or I fell behind.

"I'll give you a simple example of how I feed on her," he said, coming alongside me. "For example, she's a dancer, man, not as an occupational thing, just in the way she moves; she's a natural damn dancer and she doesn't even fucking know it." We got separated by the crowd again. He was a little annoyed when he came alongside this time. "So when I'm around her I check out the way she stands and that helps me with my stance. It helps me express the charisma I naturally possess," he said. We turned the corner onto Grove Street, where the sidewalk was far less crowded.

"The way I stand should say something more than: Is it a sexy stance? It has to say how I feel about myself." He strode a few cool steps to show me what he meant. "You see what I mean?"

"Sure," I said.

He stopped and cocked his head. "Aa-a-y-y-y-ya-a, George, you know, you're not as dumb as you look," he laughed and then took a few more cool strides. His Levi's suit was almost new and his red shirt was open at the collar, with a blue-and-red kerchief around his neck, knotted at the side, with the two loose ends thrown carelessly over his shoulder.

I waited for him to slow down. "Hey, look, one thing I've always wanted to know, why do guys who are naturally very good-looking always work so hard to be good-looking?" We reached his lady friend's apartment building.

"I don't know," he said. "I don't consider myself good-looking."

"Neither do I," I said. "I wasn't talking about you." We laughed and smacked palms before going into the downstairs hallway to ascend the four flights of stairs. Inside he fixed scotch and water for us. The apartment was amazingly bare. He was a fairly good-looking man and knew it. It was written in every move he made. He sat down on the sofa, and I sat on one of the two director's chairs against the wall.

"And uncool guys are usually happier than cool guys, anyway," I said.

"That's true, man. There's an advantage to being an ugly dude like you," he laughed.

"And the only person you love is you."

"That's right. It sounds bad, huh, me saying I'm in love with me."

"Naw," I said. By now it didn't sound bad to me.

"It's absolutely true. If I'd take you to my apartment you'd see," he said and began using his hands to talk with. He

The Mind Blower   125

turned them over and over as if he were winding his words out. "I got mirrors all over the front room and seven or eight pictures of myself scattered around the apartment.

"I have pictures of myself because they represent me at a certain time and feeling," he said. "And what they do is remind me of all the things I am. I picture myself as a diamond, man, a fucking diamond with light striking me from all sides." His fingers made gestures corresponding to the rays of light. "And I reflect whatever light happens to be hitting me at the time: dancer, poet, photographer, student, artist." He laughed. "I took most of the pictures myself, and this French chick took some of them.

"What I've tried to do is capture photographically every facet of my personality. So, basically, I'm not a vain person. I would rather describe myself as introspective at this particular time. I've got pictures that show me happy and other ones that show me depressed, and others that I can't even describe, man. I like looking at them. I live alone and I like moving around inside of me. For a while I don't want to love anyone but me.

"I've got pictures that were taken in Paris, and Paris opened up dimensions in me that I had never seen before, and I managed to capture them photographically. In Paris I wrote poems where I was free. For three months I could wake up and do whatever in the fuck I wanted to do—no wife, no family. Most people never have a period of freedom in their lives, and until you do it's ridiculous to talk about love. I loved Paris, man, because all my life I had been:

 running from one life
  running to another life
 hoping to begin anew
  to shed those skins of grief and pain
 but making one mistake
  taking with me my other brain."

He gave this poem quickly. His voice was too quick for sadness. His coolness would not allow sympathy. I could guess how difficult it would be for a woman to get close to this person behind this flow of talk.

"I had been running from one life to another by carrying the same old self with me. Now that I look back on it, I couldn't have been in love when I got married. It was a period in my life when I felt like shit. I didn't know what I wanted to do. I was nobody, man. I was on the verge of committing suicide. So I had this woman who said she loved me, so I said, 'Hey! I might just as well exhaust this possibility before I end my life.'

"So I got married, and the funny thing is that I married someone just like me in the wrong ways and just the opposite to me in the wrongs ways. I'm a Virgo, and a Virgo has to have his environment in order. He has to be able to move through his environment without too much hassle. It has to be neat and orderly. In this respect she was the opposite to me. She was a very sloppy housekeeper. You should have seen our apartment then, and then look at my apartment now. I'm a better housekeeper than she was. My wife was so-o-o-o-o disorderly. She put my shit in places where I'd have to search for hours to find it. Half the time, she didn't even know where she had put stuff. Nothing had a place, I mean a place where you could always go and find it. One week, you might find the paper towels in the linen closet and then, when you looked the next week, they'd be in the kitchen cabinet, and if they weren't there you might find them in the bathroom vanity."

Finally he relaxed and sat back on the sofa. His tone was serious and smooth. "I don't mean it was only minor annoyances. It was big things, too, but minor things are clues to the way a person's mind works. Each one of these things was just a reminder of the over-all rut we were in."

"But everything you've said," I said, "doesn't mean that you are the only person you can love. There are people whose minds work like yours. People who are not in ruts."

"But a human being is a very individualistic, a very fussy thing. I got tired of looking around for someone who was willing to work hard to please me. So I decided to work hard to please myself. Then, when I looked at how much I was willing to do for me, I began falling in love with myself. And in that way I didn't have to ask anyone for this thing that seemed so difficult for them to give. I got fed up with excuses and disappointments. I got fed up with shabbiness and halitosis and dealing with people's moods. Now when I'm in a certain mood, I can be sure that my lover is in the same mood."

"Yup. You can be sure of that," I said, and then I was instantly sorry that I had said it in that way. I didn't want him to get the idea that I was passing judgment on what he was saying. The problem was that while interviewing his wife I got the impression that she was really a very sweet person. But you never know about people until you've been around them for a while. Clarence Stafford might well be a very nice guy too. His lady friend said he was. She said he demanded a lot but gave a lot.

"I don't know," he said. "This may be a temporary state, and then again it may be permanent. I'm not going to sit here and predict. I'm going to follow the truest course I know to wherever in the hell it leads, even if it means laying up in my place alone looking at pictures of myself and masturbating. See? I'm brave enough to take it all the way to the end.

"Man, I would like it to be some other way. I would like for love to be like it is in a storybook. But I'm not going to lie about it. If it's not that way, I'm going to deal with it the way it is. I'm going to follow my feelings. Shit, for us it's not a matter of us growing up, falling in love, getting married, and living happily ever after like in a storybook.

"I don't think it's that simple for anyone, but *we* can't even pretend that it is. The truth slaps us in the face every day. It's a struggle. It's a constant struggle. It starts out as love, or something we call love, and then it becomes something else. Society says it changes, it becomes a different kind of love after a while. That's bullshit.

"It's not love at all, but society gives you this excuse for staying together by calling it a different kind of love. Society is busy telling you that you don't really feel what you know you feel. It's telling you, 'No, you're not bored. You love sitting around doing nothing. No, you're not turned off to this woman laying next to you. You just need a little alcohol to stimulate you. No, you're not restless. You just need a few tranquilizers to cool you out." He sat forward on the edge of the sofa again.

"Because, you know what happens when you stop believing society's lies? Society falls apart. But, regardless, I'm not going to be that cowardly."

"Is cowardly the right word? Is your wife a coward for staying home with the kids instead of taking off like you did?"

"She's doing what she wants to do."

"And anyway, some people get married and stay in love with each other."

"Who? Not as fast as this shit's moving out here. And anyway we weren't talking about marriage. Sure, some people get married and stay married, but that's precisely my point. How many people fall in love and stay in love? Marriage and love are two separate things.

"But you say you don't believe in either."

"No, I said I was in love with me."

"Yeah, but that was a bullshit answer."

"To your mind."

"Hey," I said. "You've got to look at some things from your wife's point of view. You're free. You got all these pictures of yourself on the wall, you can lay up and play with yourself in the mirror, but what about your children? You left your wife with two kids. How can she be free? What if she wants to lay up and play with herself?"

"Hey, man, even without kids she would be in a rut. Most people are. Maybe I'll end up in a rut. I don't know, but I've got to try. Hey, I love my kids and if I get something, if something great happens in my life financial-wise, then they're going to benefit. I'm going to be able to give those kids what my parents weren't able to give me."

"But what if it's too late? What if the kids are ruined by then? What if both your daughter and son hate you by then?"

"Hey, man, you interviewing me or harassing me?" he said angrily.

"Both," I said. I was interested to see how much fire he had in him.

"Okay," he said and looked at me for a long quiet time. Then, in a lower voice, "Do you know the answers, man?"

"No."

"I couldn't even talk with her about an answer. I actually offered to take her to Paris with me, which would have been a mistake, but I offered to take her with me. She didn't want to go. She wanted to use the money for a down payment for a home, a house, another place for us to sit in like deaf-mutes watching television, waiting to die. I mean, what good is a house if we can't even conversate. I was getting into things that she didn't know anything about: writing, photography, soul searching. My front room now is full of psychology books. She wasn't into that. She had a couple of years in college, but she never read. We were into a big alcohol thing. Drinking was all we ever did together. When we fucked, we weren't even communicating. She was down there getting hers and I was down there getting mine. She was going to school and working, and every Friday night she would buy a bottle, or three bottles, and we would drink until Monday morning, feeding each other's insecurities.

"Hey, that was it. That was me. That's how much I valued my worth. Then, one Friday night, she came home with a bottle and I said, 'I don't want to drink any more.' She was lost, man. She didn't know how else to relate to me. That signaled the end of the marriage," he said.

I looked at him as he spoke and remembered what this girl friend had said about him. She loved him, she said. She was a plain-looking girl, not nearly as pretty as I had expected. She was much sweeter than I had expected. Young, dark-skinned, soft-voiced, about nineteen, while Clarence was twenty-nine. She had been raised in a shattered home in Bed-Stuy. Clarence was her first real man. She said she loved him because he was the only man who took the time to get inside her head, and he was the only man she knew who was making a serious search for himself. She was willing to wait to see where the search ended. She hoped that it would end with her.

I got up and looked out the apartment window. The view of the narrow Village street was different from the view I later saw from the window of Clarence's apartment in the Bronx. His building was one of those cheap high-rises separated from the slums by Bruckner Expressway. Many people in New York were like him, experts at the art of makeup. In the morning they came out of crowded or barely furnished tenements looking like a million dollars. Clarence's apartment had almost no furniture in it, but the closets were full of hip clothes.

"Yeah," he said. "That's why many love relationships break up. Some people have these fantastic façades, so therefore they establish a relationship based on a weak front. See, on a certain level I operate out of a weak front. You thought you were going to get an interview out of that weak front, but I surprised you, didn't I," he said and cocked his head to the side. "Aa-a-y-y-y-ya-a! That's why I don't like to speak about love in an ordinary sense. Until you've learned how to love yourself, to put that label—I LOVE YOU—on a relationship with somebody else is just bullshit."

"How close are you to being free enough to use that label?"

"I don't know, man. I've come a long ways, but I may have a long way to go, since I started from a point of hating myself, man. I grew up with very negative opinions about myself. I didn't have a damn thing as a kid. I used to think that I was ugly. I was the only light-skinned one in my family. I wanted to be darker, like my father and my brothers. And when I was little I had a very small penis, or at least I thought I did. And I was afraid to expose my genitals. I felt like a little boy. No hair. And my older brothers used to talk about the women they were fucking and I'd say, 'Yeah, I'm fucking.' And they'd say, 'Tee-he-he, no you ain't. We saw you in the shower. You couldn't be.' I had this fantastic inferiority complex. I thought my head was too big. My nose was too big. My lips were too big, and I was very short when I was young. In gym class when they built the human pyramid, I was always the guy they put on top. I was a small cat. All my friends were taller than me all during high school. Then, in the last year of high school, a lot of things started happening. I started getting taller. In eighteen months I went from five foot four to six foot one. I started putting on weight. My dick started to get bigger.

"But I still didn't love myself. It's hard to start loving yourself after you've had so many years of having a low opinion of yourself. So I had to get married. I thought that if someone else loved me, then that would be proof that these new, high opinions of myself were really valid.

"See, what I realized about marriage is that I was looking to my wife for approval. I was looking to her to confirm these positive images of me that I only half believed in myself. She wouldn't do it. She absolutely wouldn't do it. I would bring photographs home. Pictures I had taken of various things. The kids would say, 'Daddy, that looks good' or 'Daddy, they look nice.' She wouldn't say anything. She would say, 'You forgot to get milk for the kids' breakfast.' That would be her response to my effort to gain some confirmation.

"So I stopped even asking for her approval. I started looking at the things I did in an objective manner on my own. And I would say to myself, 'If someone else had taken these pictures you would consider that person a good photographer, so why not consider yourself a good photographer? And then on my job. I was working for this cable-TV firm and I kept getting promotions, so I said to myself, 'If someone else was getting promotions like this I would consider him an all-right dude, so why not consider yourself an all-right dude?

"And I'd look in the mirror and say, "If someone else looked like you look, you'd consider that person a handsome person, so why not consider yourself a handsome person? So I got my own place and I put mirrors on the wall and I went to work on myself. I put up photographs of myself, and I put up plaques representing my achievements, even back to my report cards in elementary school. I got them laminated and I hung them on the wall and looked at them until I could really dig the fact that in elementary school I was actually a B++ student. I got to a point where I could pass myself in the mirror and say, 'I like that person' or 'I admire that person.' And then I got to a point where I could say, 'Clarence, you're a motherfucka, man. You're all right,'" he said. "'Clarence, I love you, man. I really love you,'" The Mind Blower said to himself and eased back on the sofa in his lady friend's apartment.

10

Too Much, Too Many

How many times can a body be in love?
As many times as there is time in a lifetime.

"How many times can a person be in love?" I asked.

"I don't know," she said. "I'd tell you if I knew. I don't know, though." She smiled and flapped her false eyelashes. She looked up toward the cloudy blue sky and placed her finger to the side of her lip to help herself think. "You could say I've been in love twenty times, at least. I've been in love at least twenty times," she said in her singsong voice.

I looked at her. "How old are you?"

"Twenty." She paused, pouted, and laughed.

"Yeah?" I said, knowing precisely why she laughed.

"Yup. I turned twenty this January. . . . Don't laugh; I'm serious." She poked out her bright red lips and flapped her eyelashes again. "I started when I was fourteen," she said, as if that would clear up the problem. "Yup."

"But some people call that puppy love," I said and stretched out on her blue blanket.

"I don't call it that. It's all love. I don't call any of it puppy love."

"Why not?" I asked.

"Because I'm not a puppy," she said. Laughter burst through her pout. "What right do stuffy old people have to say what is puppy love and what is people love? What right?" Her giggle said they had no right.

"I don't know," I replied and looked around at the other people lounging on the grass in Central Park. She sat erect as if on a straight-back chair. She looked as if she had practiced yoga, but hadn't. When she stood up she was tall in her faded jeans, which had been cut almost to bikini length. When she walked she moved gracefully across the rough grass in her red shoes with two-inch soles and three-inch heels. The red shoes matched her red lips. She sat back down.

Her eyes were as clear as porcelain. Her head was completely bald and shiny, like her eyelids above her inch-long lashes. "I'm serious," she said.

"But when I say love I mean spiritually, emotionally, and physically," I said.

"Shoot, when I say love I mean spiritually, emotionally, and physically, too. Love ain't love unless it involves everything. I

Too Much, Too Many   135

don't call it love unless it gets right down to the biscuit, no-o-om uh-un." She laughed, and her belly, naked below her white halter, wiggled.

"Okay. You started when you were fourteen. You're twenty now. How could you be in love twenty times in six years?"

"It might be more than twenty." She laughed. The astrological sign for Aquarius was painted on her naked belly in red lip gloss. Her shoes, belly, and lips were the same color red.

"You're a mess," I said, laughing.

"Sometimes I have three running at once. Four. If I see someone I want, I just add 'im on. Shoot." She pouted for a long time, then laughed. "I have to be in love. I can't live without love. I can't go without love. I won't allow it." She stared at me with her big, fluffy eyes. She knew that her eyes had a usable glow. People who looked at them would laugh. They twinkled there below her shiny, bald head. "Oh-o-o" she said and licked her big red lips and giggled and wiggled her skinny belly.

"How deep is the love you're talking about?"

"Very, very, very deep," she said solemnly. "I hear people say you can only love one person at a time. That's a lot of bull. You know, the most people who say that, they're Taurus people. In junior high school I was in love with this Taurus person. It was nice for a while. He was twenty-one. I was fourteen. He was the one who broke me in. I think everyone should be broken in by a Scorpio person or a Taurus person, but then you should get away from them. They try to be too domineering. Don't do that. You go your free way and I go mine, and we'll join together when you get back." She laughed her gitty giggle that exposed a cute gap between her teeth.

"You were raised in the projects on Gun Hill Road," I said.

"Yup," she said.

"Your mother told me."

"Mom, she's nice. She's a Taurus person. My second boy friend was a Taurus. He wanted to get married and have babies and other such nonsense. We were in different realms.

Then another Taurus person came into the picture—that was for about five months—and then he started getting like the other one: trying to run my life. Don't do that." She frowned. "Don't try to change me."

"Maybe they thought you were too young to know your own mind."

"Who?" she said, offended.

"You," I shot back. "You were only fourteen."

"But I've always had an old mind," she said and giggled, showing the gap between her teeth.

"So that's two. At least eighteen more and you're already almost fifteen.

"What you mean, two? That's three Tauruses and I was going with other people at the same time."

"Going with?"

"Okay, in love with. Love."

"Deeply in love?"

"Yup, deeply. I love different people for different moods. Then, when I was sixteen, I met my first Sagittarian—a go-o-o-die." She laughed and licked her lips. "Those people. You can dance all over the world with them. He was nice, but he was on drugs. You can't stay in love with a person on drugs. You're not on the same mental plane. They're slowed down, drugged down, worse than a Taurus person." She laughed. "He used to stay up all night. Worry me. He started looking bad. Sagittarians have a lot of mental problems, don't they? I've had three boy friends go on drugs. Isn't that odd?" she said absent-mindedly.

"Then came another Sagittarian. I think that's my key. Even the way it's spelled. I'm Aquarius. He's Sagittarius. The ring is nice. Some combination! I'm living with a Sagittarius person now. This could be the deepest ever. You know why? Because it's the first time I ever lived with anyone. It's nice. He gets up in the morning and goes his way, and I get up and go mine. He doesn't try to tag along behind me, thank God."

"So love and freedom have to go together?"

"They *have* to. They just have to. That's what love is: free-

Too Much, Too Many 137

dom for each person to do his thing." Her face grew serious. It was a smooth face. Walnut brown—lighter than the wood, darker than the nut.

I had met the guy she was living with. He was a tall man with a big Afro, who stalked the streets of New York with a multilens camera slung around his neck. So far as I knew, he didn't work. But New York was like that. Central Park was like that: full of work-age adults. Some had left their offices for lunch and had not returned; some were, like Michelle, pleasantly unemployed and stylishly impoverished, but apparently unworried. They had found a way to live.

She leaned back. We looked around the park. "So you call this madness love?" I asked.

"Yup; what else is love?"

"Jealousy, passion, companionship."

"That's what you say it is." She was looking toward the footbridge.

"That's what I heard," I said.

"From who?" she asked in mock anger.

"From everybody."

"Except me," she said and stretched.

"What do you do all day?"

"Enjoy my life." She laughed. "People like me. Men like me. I've never been in love with a man I couldn't get. Every man I fall for, I get. If . . . you . . . uh . . . yeah! Shoot. If I want you I get you." She laughed. "No man has *ever* turned me down. I've had to turn a few down, though. I had to. I don't have time to love everybody."

"You know I'm not talking about sex," I said.

"I'm not talking about sex either." She pouted. We remained silent and watched a shirtless hippie try to bring a shaggy dog down the side of a giant gray boulder. The dog was frightened because his claws wouldn't take hold even though he was moving sideways. He slid frantically until he was close enough to the bottom to jump.

"I have to feel a person's spirit before I even get involved sexually, before I even want to be with a man, but then if I

138   *Love, Black Love*

want him I get him. Men like my lips," she said. "They say I have big, kissable lips." She licked her big, kissable lips. She had licked them so much that the lip gloss had faded. Her lips were now the same shade of red as the heart-shaped patches all over her bikini-cut, faded jeans.

"But the funny thing is: I don't like to kiss. Men want to get hold of my lips, but I don't really like to kiss. Isn't that odd? If he wants to kiss, I'll kiss; but if you kiss me on the neck, I love it." She pouted and laughed.

"I don't like to be kissed in the ear. My neck, o-o-ow, yup. The right side more so than the left side. It just . . . feels good." She stuck her tongue out and laughed.

"But my tongue. It's very sensitive. That's why I stick it out. Catch the breeze. Not to stimulate my lips but to rub my tongue on my lips, Um-m-m-m." She stuck out her tongue again and rubbed her bald head.

"When do you think you'll settle down and get married?" I asked.

She snapped her tongue back in as if I had cursed her. "Married?"

"Yeah."

"What is marriage? It isn't anything. It has nothing to do with love. It has no value to me. If it's to have children, I can have children without being married," she said. She began to tell me how much her mother hated to hear her talk like that. Her mother believed in marriage. I knew her mother. In fact, it was her mother who had first told me that I should talk to Michelle. "That child's crazy. She's just like her Daddy," she'd said. Michelle's mother lived alone, still in the projects where she had raised her five daughters. She was still very good friends with Michelle's father, even though they had been separated for fifteen years.

Michelle's father was a playboy, but he had always been good about supporting his family. His daughter loved him. Michelle even looked like him, her mother had said. "My father told me never let a man support me. I wouldn't do that. I can take care of myself. If I had a child, I could take care of that child, too. I don't see where . . . shoot . . . no. My oldest sister warned me: Never get married. She's married. She should know.

"Most women get married for material things. You'd be surprised. They call it love. They even talk themselves into believing, really believing they're in love, but they're really after the material things. I don't worry about things like that. I can do without a lot of money. There's a man in the Bronx right now, with quite a bit of money, who wants to take care of me, and give me money. He's a nice man. I like to talk to him, but something about him don't strike me right." She frowned playfully.

"How do you know when you're in love?" I asked and looked away, toward the boulder where the dog had slid down.

"It's easy. Something clicks. You can be with a person and something clicks, then you know. You just get that certain feeling when you're with that person. I could never be with a man, no matter what he has, if I didn't get that certain feeling."

"Some people call that infatuation," I said looking back at her smooth face, with the fluffy playful eyes.

"It's not infatuation. It's love, because I'm talking about a spiritual, mental, emotional and physical click." She laughed. "I'm not talking about someone just coming up to you on the street and you getting that feeling. I'm talking about setting down and sharing some time, and you being there because of the way that person makes you feel. It may start from infatuation, but it's more than that. It's love. Love is a click." She clicked her tongue against the roof of her mouth and laughed. "I'm serious," she said. "It's a click."

I laughed and looked away from her again. A crowd had gathered on the small hill near the footbridge. And I was thinking about how, the previous summer, I had seen two policemen in big shoes chasing a barefoot teen-ager across that hill. The park was crowded then. The policemen couldn't overtake the boy. One policeman was screaming, "Shoot the bastard, shoot the bastard." The other one was running, holding his hat in one hand and firing his pistol into the air with the other.

Suddenly the first policeman dropped to one knee and leveled his gun. People scattered. Others hit the dirt, screaming. The teen-ager disappeared under the footbridge before the policeman got off a shot.

"I have to be in love. It wakes my whole nature up. I don't see how people live without love. There's never a time when I'm not in love."

"How many people do you love now?"

"Only three."

"Only three."

"Yup. Why do people feel that love has to be something drugged down, with one person hanging onto the other?

"I don't know.

"I always like to have a fresh love happening and an old, comfortable love going, and a spare. I think three's my magic number."

"Which one do you love most?"

"I don't compare one man to another. You'll just mess yourself up by comparing one man to another. But I like the way new love feels. I like the process of getting to know more about a person. I like discovering things about him. I like the anticipation when I'm on my way to see him or waiting somewhere to meet him. It makes you tingle. It's hard to wait, too. That's how you can tell if you're in love."

"But how can you be giving yourself totally to three men at the same time?"

"Not the same time; you might see one in the morning, one in the afternoon, and one in the evening," she laughed, making fun of my question. "When you love one man, he don't use up the love. You still have it to give. Shoot! Sometimes he just makes it better for the next man, because he puts you in a receptive mood."

"Of course, you're talking about sex."

"No. You the one keep talking about that," she said. "I'm not a sex fiend."

Too Much, Too Many   141

"How much does looks—physical appearance—matter to you?"

"That could be very important. Love could start from that. From the way a person looks. You wouldn't want to be with someone ugly, or someone weird-looking," she said, rubbing her head. "I like tall men. And I always look at a man's eyes. His eyes tell you a lot about his insides. They tell you what plane he's living on, and then something inside you tells you if you want to live on that plane with him for a while. I could never love a man with dead eyes. I like slender men, but sometimes I've been in love with a husky man."

"I guess in twenty times there'd have to be at least a couple husky men," I said sarcastically.

She looked at me as if to say, you should be ashamed of making fun of me. I'm being serious and you're being sarcastic. "But I've never seen a fat man who's sexy."

"We're not talking about sex," I said.

"How can it be love if it doesn't involve sex?"

"True, but I'm not talking about sex primarily," I said.

"I'm not talking about that, either. People get the wrong idea. They think when I say free, I mean free love. The truth is, and this is the truth, I'm not that dominated by sex. I go for weeks without sex. Me and my man sleep together many nights without sex. I love him because he has this fabulous free spirit, the spirit of an explorer. I have fun with him. We laugh together and do crazy things. Isn't it odd that most people think that love has to be some awful, painful thing—"

"So you've never been hurt in love, then."

"Oh, yes, I've been hurt. When this guy I loved, Clarence, went on drugs, that hurt. I cried. I begged him. I sat up at night with him wondering why he was killing himself like that. I went away, saying I never wanted to see him again, and came back to try some more to make him stop. I loved him because he was struggling to *be*, struggling to *be*, but his struggle was taking him places where I didn't like to see him go. He messed up my whole cycle. I was in love with two other men at this time and I couldn't be with them for worrying about Clarence. He was very sensitive. He was too sensitive, Clarence. When the world hurt, Clarence hurt. Every man I've ever loved had the potential to go off in some way. Every man has been a searcher."

"Everyone in the world's searching."

"No, some of them give up and settle for what they got, and some react in different ways to life forces. I have to dig the way you react to life forces, and then I feel like I want to be with you. I want to spend time with you. I want to call you when I'm in the mood you're in, and laugh with you and make love to you if that's what we decide. That's why I believe in compatibility as far as astrological signs is concerned. I didn't use to believe in it so strong, but I've found it is true in nearly every case, so I believe. I don't believe in it to the extent that I would let astrology run my life, but I believe in it to the extent that I tend to avoid people under certain signs:

"Taurus. They're too level. One day just like the next. Chomp, chomp, chomp." She swung her body from side to side like someone marching. "My life goes up and down, polka dots and stripes and circles and all. But Taurus people are very attracted to me. I have to run from them.

"Pisces, they try to cuddle up to you. I like certain people to cuddle up to me, but I don't want certain other people to cuddle up to me. You can understand my position, can't you? If I don't invite you to cuddle up to me, don't." She smacked at an imaginary cuddler.

"Geminis, my sister is a Gemini and one of my last boy friends was a Gemini. I get along with them okay. They're crazy, you know? All of them. This Gemini I had liked to boogaloo all the time. He stayed in one spot. He didn't want to broaden out.

"Capricorns, they're people collectors. They like you to belong to them. They like to own people. You can't be their friend and be the friend of someone they don't like. Why are people like that? Isn't it odd?" she asked sincerely. "They can tell you about yourself, though, Capricorns. They set around and watch you and then they'll tell you about yourself.

Too Much, Too Many 143

"Aries, they're very rough. There're two of them hunting around New York for me now. One in a green Oldsmobile. Whenever I see a green Oldsmobile, I run. They charge behind you so they can grab you." She pretended to be grabbing out at someone. Then she switched parts and began swinging at an imaginary Aries: "Get out of here. Leave me alone. They're sweet, though, but I have to dodge them. They like to tell you what they're going to do to you, what they're going to get from you. . . . Not from me," she spoke again to the imaginary Aries. "I make the decision about who I let have me." She blinked furiously and burst into laughter.

"Cancers. Their feelings get hurt too easily. You can stand there and pet them sometimes, but you can't do that all your life. You can't," she said as if I didn't believe her. "That's why I have to keep moving. You can't spend your entire life petting them," she said. Having run through about half of the zodiac, she stopped. I assume, then, that the rest of the Zodiac was fine. We watched a couple coming across the footbridge holding hands.

"Then, how many times, do you think, a body can fall in love in a lifetime?" I asked her after a while.

She said distinctly, "As many times as there is time in a lifetime."

11

Maria Winston

I asked, "Can true, deep love exist without jealousy?"
and she said without hesitating, "Yes; ask Maria Winston."

It is warm when she comes down from the forty-seventh floor of the gray Manhattan skyscraper where she works. A stream of people come out with her. Her green sweater is slung carelessly across her shoulder. She walks as if barefooted. Her brown nose sweats a little when she gets into the front seat. She smiles. She is forever smiling.

She doesn't speak. Her mouth forms the word "Hello" and her smile says she is friendly. Strange little girl. She is so small that when she sits back on the seat her feet won't touch the rubber floor mat.

I start uptown with her in the rush of New York traffic. Rude taxis dart like yellow beetles from lane to lane along Park Avenue. No, she doesn't mind talking. Yes, she believes in love.

I make a joke about her size. She doesn't reply, but smiles. I tell her that her friend said she is strange. She still does not respond. She is too busy smiling.

"It's very hard to be in love," I say.

"Yes," she says. It's easy to forget that she has been in New York for more than three years and that she works at a rather sophisticated job in a financial management firm. The speed of New York seems not to have changed her. I had talked to her the day before. I remember that when she is ready she will begin to talk. I go over and get on Madison Avenue, where the traffic lights are timed so that if you drive at a certain speed you can move uptown without stopping. I turn left, go one block facing the sun low over Central Park, and then turn northward.

She is from Mississippi. She still hot-combs her hair. It is in a bang across her smooth forehead. I say: "I was interviewing this lady who said she had been in love twenty times. Do you think a person can be in love that many times in a lifetime?"

She says she doesn't know. She doesn't want to get into anybody's story. She only wants to tell her own.

"How many times have you been in love?"

"Only once," she says.

"You still in love?"

"I'll always be," she says. She smiles shyly. It's easy to forget

Maria Winston   147

the little slivers of brilliance that slip into her conversation to show that she is much, much smarter than she wants people to believe. "I will always love Mr. Winston," she said.

Her name is Maria Winston. She calls her husband Mr. Winston because she thinks of him as Mr. Winston. He lives with her girl friend, her other friend told me. He is her husband and he lives with a girl who she gave him to make him happy in his old age.

"You're very shy," I say.

"I know," she replies, smiling. Her smile is without tension, her personality seems too calm for passion. She seems like one of those children who run away from vaguely unpleasant homes to join cults, and are taught how to smile. She has been taught how to smile, her other girl friend told me yesterday.

"She get's on my nerves," the girl friend has said.

"Why?"

"She's a very intelligent person, but she lets her husband use her. She gets on my nerves. She acts like a Moonie. That's who she acts like, one of those people who worship Rev. Sun Myung Moon," her friend had said.

"Is Mr. Winston an Oriental?" I asked playfully.

"No, he's a nigger," her friend had said.

The ride uptown on Madison Avenue is faster than it would have been on Park; not as many cabs.

"Mr. Winston must have a knack for picking women of a certain type," I say as I turn onto Eighty-fifth Street. The light is red at the end of the block.

She says: "No. . . . No, because I wasn't like this when he found me. He taught me how to be happy. That's why I wanted to talk to you, so I could tell people that love can teach you how to be happy. He trained all his ex-wives and girl friends to be like this regardless of what they were before."

We cross Fifth Avenue into the park, heading toward the West Side.

"How many ex-wives did he have?"

"Three."

"And ex-girl friends?"

"I don't know. What I wanted to say is, you have to let love be what it is. You just can't try to make it be what it won't be. Love is making a person happy and being happy yourself. I was just the opposite. I was a very selfish person. I was a tomboy, always fighting the other children. I hated everyone and everything, and I would've been like that the rest of my life. I would've had a miserable existence. So that's why I would do anything for Mr. Winston's happiness. He didn't ask me for my friend. I saw him looking at her and I used to tease him about her, and he got to know her and like her. He's a very special person, so I gave her to him." She laughs at my perplexity.

"You're a strange little woman," I say.

She doesn't respond with anything other than her mischievous smile. After a long moment of silence she says, "I guess you don't believe in love so strong that you want the person you love to have anything that person wants?"

"I've heard of it. I've heard women say, 'I'll do anything for my man,' but I've never seen it practiced. I didn't even know the phrase could be taken literally. No one is willing to do absolutely anything for another person."

"Of course not absolutely anything, but there are people who will do much, much more than others who claim they would do anything."

"True, some people who say it are talking only about a few conventional things. Maybe no more than fix a person's food or keep a person's house, or give a person money, or something like that. Easy things."

"For some people, giving is never easy," she says. She is serious for a moment.

"Is what you give easy?"

She smiles. "Yes. It started as a joke, but I would do a great deal for him. I want him to retire one day. That's why I work so hard: so I can have money to help him retire. Other women, his ex-wives and ex-girl friends, will help him," she says.

Maria Winston   149

"Amazing," I say as we come up the hill toward Central Park West. "Then, the man to talk to about love is Mr. Winston."

"Oh, he would never talk to you about that. He's friendly, but he never talks about that. He knows I'm talking to you, but when I asked him he said he doesn't know anything about love. He said he just likes to be good to people, that's all."

The day before, I had had in mind a picture of a deeply spiritual man, a recluse of sorts, but Maria had told me I was wrong. He is an economist who goes to work in downtown Manhattan each day. He is neither rich nor poor. He is just an average man.

"That's why it's hard to tell about people in New York," I say. "You see them walking in the streets looking like nothing special, and you can never guess how different each might be from the other, never guess what twists and turns the human heart takes in response to what strange features of background or necessity. People can be almost anything. People are almost anything," I say thinking that Maria, for example, had been very rich once and had had a strange background. About her there was a look of something different, but who could have guessed whether love, hate, loneliness, fear, selfishness, Lesbianism, cocaine, makeup, adrenalin, hay fever, pregnancy, Jesus, or life itself was what gave her her special glow?

Her life has always been different, she says. It was very different even back when she was a hate-filled child in Mississippi. And then there had been the other thing: the marriage to Mr. Winston, who was married to her for two years before he made love to her.

"Would you like something to eat?" I ask, thinking of a hamburger place farther up Broadway, near Columbia.

"All right," she says.

"How old is he?" I ask.

"He's fifty-eight."

"And you?"

"Twenty-three."

"So, how old were you when you married him?"

"I was fifteen."

"Fifteen?"

"Fifteen." The whole thing is very amusing to her. She seems to like to shock people with the uniqueness of her life. We go into the Hamburger Gourmet and stand in line behind a Spanish woman with her head wound and tied in dark silk. She is with a man in green, shapeless polyester pants. Hunger causes my stomach to hurt a little.

"Is he happy?" I ask.

"I think he is content. That would be a better word for it: content." She smiles her Sun Myung Moon smile.

"Were you afraid at fifteen to be married?"

"I was afraid. Fifteen is very young, and I had been mostly a tomboy before that. I was afraid that I wouldn't be able to cook for him, or clean his house in the proper way. I had never done this. I had always had a maid. I lived with a very wealthy white family as a child."

I frown in disbelief. I knew that she was wealthy, but I didn't know that the family she lived with was white. I begin to wonder, where are all these strange circumstances coming from?

"They gave me everything I wanted," she says. "They had a black woman to clean my room for me. I had a maid to do everything for me, but Mr. Winston told me that he would teach me to do everything for him."

"But were you afraid of the sexual part of marriage?"

"Oh, yes, I was." We move forward to the counter. I order a cheeseburger. She wants only french fries and a coke.

"You were a virgin."

"Yes, oh, yes." This time, she blushes. The counter girl brings our order. We go upstairs to eat.

"Then, you were afraid of that?"

"Yes, but he talked to me and told me not to be afraid of being a real wife, because at first I was not supposed to be a real wife. He was going to teach me how to be happy. We didn't make love, ever, for the first two years. We slept in the same room but we didn't sleep together. He just wanted to marry me to teach me how to be happy and how to stop hat-

Maria Winston   151

ing everything and fighting. The white people, they didn't want me to get married at first, but finally they thought it was best that I move away from them, so they let me marry him so he could take care of me," she says and seems to want to say more but doesn't, even though she now knows I suspect that there is more to this than she has so far said.

"They were very wealthy?" I ask.

"Yes, they owned a lot of stores. They sent me to private school in Alabama. They lived in Mississippi. . . ."

"You've had a very different life. Is that why you look at love so differently?"

"Do I look at it differently? I want what everybody wants: to be happy. That's what everybody wants."

"By racial composition, what are you?" I ask.

"My mother is half black, half Indian; my father is half white and half black. I don't know. I think my father's father was white. I don't know my father very well. He left my mother when I was a baby, and then she married this man with twelve children."

"Did you like being married at first?"

"No. I was afraid, because I liked to go and play. In the summertime I liked to play all the time, and I was afraid that by being married I would have to stay in the house and do the housework. But Mr. Winston, he let me go out to play with the other children. He is a very nice man." A glow comes into her voice when she talks about Mr. Winston. She glows and smiles.

"And you're sure that he would not let me interview him?"

Her brow wrinkles. "No, he'd never." She laughs as if it is ridiculous to want to talk to Mr. Winston, her husband.

The next day, we sit in my car at the corner of 100th Street and Broadway and watch Mr. Winston walking toward home. It is nearly six P.M. Dust hangs in the air, but he is not of the dust. He parts the dust and evening as the prow of a boat parts the water. He is what people mean when they say, "a fine old man," but thin, fleshless. His clothing is expensive and too British for this Hispanic neighborhood, and too tailored and warm for a spring day. She loves him. She smiles, embarrassed, watching him on his way to his apartment, where her girl friend is likely to be waiting supper for him. She doesn't know what to say, so she keeps on smiling. Her embarrassment seems to be based on the fact that now, for the first time, we are seeing him in the flesh after having talked about him so much. "There he is," she announces. It's all a joke to her.

"You sure he wouldn't consent to an interview?"

"No, no, you know what? When I told him, he said for me to go ahead but that he didn't believe in love." She laughs.

"Is that true?"

"No, he believes in it. He believes in being good to people. And that's what love is."

"Does he love you?"

"Yes, he does," she says. "He took the time with me to change my life."

"Does he love your girl friend?"

"Yes, he loves everybody," she says. We watch him in the distance go up the steps into the brownstone where he lives on the first floor. We get out of the car and walk up Broadway, talking. She says she has to go soon, go to her real mother's house in the Bronx. She is staying with her real mother. Her real mother doesn't like Mr. Winston. She refuses to acknowledge that he is really her husband.

"She was under age," the real mother said. "And I didn't give that old man permission to marry my daughter." Her mother has been in New York longer than Maria. Her mother moved up seven years ago with the man she married after Maria's father ran off. She, the man, and his twelve children had been living in the Bronx for seven years.

Maria claimed that her mother was not really married either, since she had never gotten a divorce from Maria's father. Maria had hated her stepfather and his twelve children. She had hated the children because her mother had favored them over her even though eleven of them were older than she.

Maria always used to fight them, and though she was younger, she always won the fights, because she was wilder and more evil. They would make her cry, but she would pick up anything she could get her hands on and hit them. One of the boys, three years older than Maria, had a long, infected cut over his eye from Maria's attempt to knock his eye out with a piece of iron.

The children had said it was her Indian blood, and they let her alone. She had hated living with them, so she'd been given away to a white family that her mother had once worked for.

These people, the Knowleses had lived in a big Colonial house just outside Jackson, Mississippi. Maria had it made. They'd had enough money to give her anything she wanted. She'd started school in the colored school system of Jackson. They'd hired a driver to take her in and pick her up.

To the other black kids she was a mystery, this little girl who showed up every day in a car. She shied away from them, and the more unhappy she became the more things the Knowleses bought for her to make her happy. She had everything, she says.

We get two fish sandwiches and sit eating them, in the Hamburger Gourmet again. We watch the Columbia University students come in and rush out to their evening classes. We can hear the hum of the Xerox machines in the copy shop next door. Outside, traffic rushes by in the failing light.

"You should have seen me," she says. "I was a wild child. I started to do devilish things. I didn't think about other people's feelings. I would get a stick and chase people's cows into the woods. I would set fires. They were harmless little fires, but I would set them and then watch people panic to put them out. And fight! I'd fight if another child even looked at me the wrong way. And though I was small I always won, no matter if I was bleeding or not." She stirs her coke with her drinking straw.

"But I was very friendly toward adults, black or white. It was as if I held all adults in awe because they knew something that I had to find out about in order to live."

"My stepparents had to send me away to a boarding school because I fought so much. I did well in boarding school. I was very smart. I always got the best grades in my classes. I graduated high school at fourteen, but, each year, the nine months I spent at boarding school wasn't even like living. I just waited for the summer, so I could run wild and play on my stepparents' farm.

"I liked to do things that boys like to do: climb trees, sneak out of the house at night and go fishing. I never wore a dress except when I had to," she says. "I had a dog, just like a little boy."

I wondered if she is worrying at all about Mr. Winston and her girl friend, but she says no. "I don't think about it. I gave the girl to him. I told her things to do to be good to him, how to fix his food and make him happy." She laughs. "Then I went to stay at my mother's house, because my mother is sick and not expected to live and she needs me to take care of her. Everyone else left her."

"What if he wants to marry your girl friend?" I ask.

"Then I would divorce him and let him marry her. If that's what he wants. I would want that to make him happy."

"Then, how can it be love if you can give him up so easily?"

"It won't be easy," she says and looks at the side of her coke cup to see how much more she has to drink before she has nothing left but ice. A small Chinaman in a white shirt comes up the stairs. He sits at a table near the window and eats a dark sausage on a long roll.

"What if he never wants to see you again, or to be with you again?"

"That would hurt, but he would never do that. He loves me very much. I feel sure of his love," she says calmly.

"Do you think you'll ever fall in love with anyone else?"

"Yes, I could," she says just as calmly. "I could fall in love very easily now that I know how to love." She looks at me, enjoying my confusion. "See, there's something I didn't tell you about why my husband married me. I am almost like a daughter to him. Often I feel like a daughter to him. He married me to take me out of my stepparents' house, and the only way he could do that was to marry me. I didn't tell you that," she says. "I didn't tell you the full story. I intentionally wanted to confuse you for the fun of it.

Maria Winston   155

"When I graduated high school, I passed the entrance examination to go to Vanderbilt, and my stepfather was going to send me, but they thought I should wait out a year so I would be fifteen, almost sixteen. So for a year I waited around the house, and in that year things happened which led to my marriage." She is serious now and a little nervous. The Chinaman finishes his sausage, wipes his hands carefully, and leaves.

"As I say, at the time, I considered myself a tomboy, and my stepparents wanted to make a little lady out of me. You know: make me more ladylike.

"They sent me to music teachers and dance teachers in Jackson, and they made me start wearing dresses, and then I noticed that my stepfather stopped looking at me like I was a daughter. One night, he came home drunk and I was in the house alone, and he came to my room and tried to kiss me.

"I'm not saying that he was a bad man. They were always very good to me. When my stepfather came into my room and tried to kiss me, I told him that I loved him as a father and I had always looked on him as a father, a real father, because he was the only father I had had.

"He apologized and left, and nothing happened with him for a long time, but I noticed his brothers, my uncles, would accidentally come into a room while I was changing clothes. They would look at me. I was embarrassed. I didn't completely understand, because I had no sexual feelings at all at that time. I was more like a little boy.

"Then, during the summer, we were out on the lake on my uncle's boat, and I had almost forgotten about the incident between me and my father. I had on my little bikini and my father told me to get on his shoulders so he could dive in the water like that. We dived in like that, and while we were under the water he tried to kiss me between my legs. I was so shocked I took water into my nose and the people on board the boat had to pull me in.

"I don't know how much his wife saw, but I know that her sister told her at that time I was getting too big to be in the house with her husband. Later, my stepmother told me this and it hurt me very much. After that, I didn't like to go in the house, because I loved my stepmother very much and what she told me had hurt me.

"A little before that, I had met Mr. Winston. He was a high school teacher who went to the same church I went to, sometimes. He always used to talk to me to try and tell me things. He would always ask me, 'Why are you always so unhappy, little girl?' He was a nice man, so when I needed someone to talk to, he was the only person I knew. I talked to him one Sunday. I told him everything that had happened, and I told him that I was going to run away to my real mother, who was in New York.

"Then, as I began to tell him about my mother and how I didn't even know for sure what part of New York she lived in, he told me that I shouldn't go to New York. Then I started staying at his apartment even when he wasn't at home, and I would pretend that he was my husband and that he had gone out to work and that we had three children but they were all sleeping. I just stayed around his apartment watching television and pretending, because I didn't want to go home.

"I told him how much I wanted to get out of my house, and he told me that the only legal way he could get me out of the house was if he married me. He didn't exactly ask me to marry him, but I went back and asked my stepparents for permission. They were very angry with me and with him. They told me no.

"Then, one night, my stepfather and mother came to my room. They had both been crying. He said, 'Maria, I don't like this marriage proposal from this old man. We have loved you and wanted only the best for you, but I feel that if you continue in this house it will cause trouble between me and my wife. To be honest, I have admitted that I no longer look at you as a daughter. You are a woman, a desirable woman.'

"I started to cry. You can imagine how I felt, me looking and feeling like a little boy and he telling me this in front of my stepmother. You can imagine how hurt I was. My stepmother said, 'Maria, we both love you very much, believe me, but we have checked and found that Mr. Winston will be a very good husband.'

Maria Winston   157

"I kept crying. They wanted to comfort me, but I didn't want either of them to touch me, two people who had meant so much to me, who had touched me and bathed me as a little naked child. Now I wanted to spit on either of them who came near me.

"I screamed for them to get out of my room. They left, but it wasn't really my room. It was theirs. I couldn't pack my clothes, because everything I owned belonged to them.

"I didn't want to give up all the luxury. They came back into the room to try to explain things. They had been crying. When I think back on it, I'm sure they really loved me. They pleaded with me. They tried to make me understand that they loved me, but this only made me sicker. The meat on my bones had come from food they had bought for me. The blood in my veins had come from the care they had given me. I felt dirty inside and out. I felt like nothing.

"I ran out of the house. That's how I came to live with Mr. Winston. He was really the only friend I had, and I felt sorry for him because he seemed poor compared to what I had. I hated most people and didn't think about their feelings, but Mr. Winston was the only person I ever felt sorry for.

"We got married in a few days. It was not a big wedding. Nobody came. It was just supposed to be a legal thing. I wasn't afraid when it happened. I didn't even think about it as a wedding, or anything like that.

"I think what he really wanted to do was teach me how to love other people and stop thinking only of myself. He would teach me how to have faith in other people and how to care about other people's problems and how to feel sad when people around me were sad. His friends would come around and he would make me listen to their problems, and after they'd go he'd show me why I should feel sympathy.

"Most people would refer to me as his daughter. They didn't know about the wedding, and because of our ages and because of the way he treated me, they would refer to me as his daughter.

"We slept in the same room, but not in the same bed. After a few months my sexual nature grew. I told him that I didn't want to be his wife in name only, but he always refused to talk about that. He said I was like a daughter to him and that he was going to send me away to college to live in the dormitory. We used to joke and flirt sometimes, but that was only to make me happy. But the more he teased me the more determined I was to be his wife. I now began to love him.

"He'd say, 'Maybe one day you'll find a younger man to love.' It was like he was ashamed to think of me as his wife. Or maybe it was something else. Maybe it was because he was getting older. I don't know. I've never been good at knowing what other people feel or knowing why other people do the things they do. In that way you can see that I've been basically self-centered. I only think of what I feel, and at that time I only wanted to be his wife in full, not just in name. I started changing my clothes in front of him. He thought all this was done in innocence, but I knew exactly what I was doing.

"But I didn't understand his feelings. I didn't understand why he would get up and leave sometimes and not come back until I was asleep. I knew he had other women that he would go to, and I hated them, but all the time he was teaching me not to hate anybody.

"Then, one time, I was in the shower and I had left my soap and face cloth in the other room. I had done this purposely so I would have to ask him to bring them to me. He tried to hand them through the door without coming in the bathroom, but I asked him to wash my back. I was seventeen, almost eighteen. He came in and washed my back and I could see that he was really afraid. I didn't care.

"By now I loved him very much. It was better than love, because he was also my friend and teacher. So I told him that I was his wife and I didn't want him seeing other women. He said I was his daughter. I cursed him and he started to spank me but I laughed and called him an old man. He couldn't spank me. I cursed at him. He wanted to treat me like a child, but he was embarrassed to try to grab me to spank me again, so he left the house.

"That was the first time I ever really felt anyone else's sadness enough to cry. When I was very young I used to cry when I was sad, but after that the only time I cried was when I was mad or when I got hurt in a fight, but it was always for me. That was the first time I cried for someone else.

"After that, I said I would stop wanting what I wanted and settle for being his daughter. I started in college at Jackson State. I made up my mind that I wanted to be an elementary-school teacher. I don't know why. I had never liked kids, but I took courses in elementary education.

"We were going along okay, but then, one time, this boy asked Mr. Winston if he could take his daughter to the movies. The boy was a boy from college who drove me home. Of course, he had no way of knowing that Mr. Winston was my husband, so my husband said yes, and I was mad at my husband for saying yes, so I stayed out very late. When I got home he was very mad. He accused me of being selfish for not coming home and fixing his supper.

"I said, 'I fixed your supper. It's on the stove.'

"He said: 'I taught you better than that. What do you want me to do, eat it off of the stove?'

"He was angrier than I had ever seen him, so I got angry. 'I don't care if you eat it off the floor,' I said.

"'How can you say that, after all I've done for you?' he yelled.

"'I didn't ask you to do anything for me,' I yelled.

"'You are my wife,' he said.

"I told him to go to hell. My old temper came back. He is a very strong man, but I didn't care if he hit me. I kept yelling at him. He took me across his knee and spanked me, but my old evil Indian blood came back and I promised myself that I wouldn't cry or move or yell out. He spanked me and when he saw he wasn't getting anywhere, he took my jeans off to spank me, but still I wouldn't cry, and then I realized that he wasn't hitting me hard. He was too afraid of hurting me. I could feel how gentle and good this man was by the little baby licks he was giving me, calling himself 'wearing me out.' The licks weren't even hard enough to make a six-year-old cry. It was funny, in a way. He was making all this noise and scolding me something terrible: 'Now maybe you'll mind. Now maybe you'll behave yourself.' He was saying stuff like this. It was really funny, but I didn't want to laugh at him. Then he stood up with this mean expression on his face. 'There. That'll show you I mean business. And there's plenty more where that came from,' he yelled.

"I had to run in the bathroom to keep from laughing in his face, because, in a way, I wanted to hold him rather than laugh at him, because, in a way, I was a rougher person than he was, and he was so good. He didn't have the will to hurt anyone.

"I stayed in the bathroom thinking about him. Soon he came to the door and asked me, 'Did I hurt you? If you wasn't so evil I wouldn't have spanked you so hard,' he said, and stormed out of the apartment. When he came back, I had a beautiful supper ready for him. He told me that I couldn't go out with that same boy again. I told him that he would have to let me become his wife. So gradually we did become husband and wife. That's why we left Jackson to come to New York. He didn't want my college friends to know that I was married to this old man."

Maria and I come out onto Broadway. Full night has come and it is cooler. We walk all the way back to where my car is parked, on the one-way street that leads down in front of Mr. Winston's apartment. We drive past. The windows to his apartment are lighted. He works as a computer supervisor for an accountancy firm downtown, and he reads and watches television when he gets home in the evening.

"You're not jealous that your girl friend might be there with him?"

"She's there. I saw her car parked across the street."

"You're not jealous."

"No," she says and smiles her Sun Myung Moon smile. We turn north on the service road alongside Riverside Drive. "I want him to be happy with my friend. She loves him very much. She is very different than I was. She has two children."

"Do you ever see Mr. Winston any more?"

"Oh, yes, he's still my husband. I see him."

"Is he still in love with you?"

"Yes, even more so. When I visit him in his office he wants to lock the door and make love to me right there. He taught me how to make love to him too well, and now he wants me to make love to him even in his office. He taught me all positions and all ways, to be even freer than a prostitute. I love to make love with him. When I go to his apartment we can't even get a meal cooked for making love." She laughs.

We come into the Bronx by the Alexander Hamilton Bridge and turn onto the Major Deegan Expressway northbound. "Sometimes he doesn't want to let me go, but I have to go up and take care of my mother, who is ill."

"How old is your friend?"

"She's thirty-nine. All of my friends are older than I am." We park in front of a small apartment building just off White Plains Road. She gets out and goes in to where her mother lives.

12
What's Wrong?

If there is something to fear, then why not be afraid?

"I love," he said, "I love fried chicken." He laughed so hard he almost fell off his seat. I had thought it funny too, the first time I heard it. The first instance had been in a conversation in the Bronx and it had come from a man so cynical that probably the only thing he could love was something to put in his stomach. He certainly couldn't love. "Not another human being down here on this planet," he had said.

Billy Fowler wasn't like that. He seemed a soft guy. "Chicken's the only thing you love, huh?"

"No, watermelon." He burst out laughing again. Tears came to his eyes.

"Yeah, but you know what I'm talking about."

"Yeah, yeah, seriously. I was in love once. Yeah, I can say I was in love one time, when I was nineteen." He had finished laughing at his jokes, but his voice was still playful. "That's all I needed. One time. I was in love with a nice girl, man. Beautiful, sensitive, affectionate, all that. So I can't complain about that part. She was great. I loved her and I'm sure she loved me, but I broke it up, intentionally.

"I messed with her head every chance I got, because I wanted to break it up. No, I can't say I did it intentionally, but when I think back on it, I knew I must have had this subconscious desire to get her away from me. Thinking back on it, what I realize is that I'm afraid of love.

"So, yeah, I'm afraid of love. I did things to her like bring other women to parties where I knew she'd be, make a fool of her in front of her friends. I did some raunchy stuff to her. She was too close to me, man. I could feel her inside my head sometimes. I loved her too much. Thinking about the power she had over me gave me some scary, uncomfortable feelings.

"Love, that's all she wanted was love. And when I was around her that's all I wanted. So I had to get away from her, because I had goals in life. I wanted to finish college. I wanted to come to New York.

"I know to this day if I had let myself love her I would be right down there in Baltimore now driving a truck or doing some other menial job to support those eight children that we used to talk about having. We used to just dream about that,

What's Wrong?   165

man, getting married and having eight children. We had names for all of them, and we had hopes for all of them. Sometimes after we made love we would lay-up just dreaming about our soon-to-be children. It was crazy, man." He pulled out his wallet and showed me a picture of a cute brown-skinned girl of about eighteen.

"I keep this picture and sometimes I wonder what happened to her. I know she's married to someone else. I know she refuses to see me. In a way, I don't blame her. I did promise to marry her, but in the end I got afraid. Not because I was afraid of marriage per se. I was just afraid of having someone in control of my emotions."

At the counter, we had both gotten steak sandwiches. He put a disgusting amount of catsup on his. I laughed. We looked out the window for a moment. "I don't want to love anybody," he said. "Not right now. When I date a woman who I could love, I'll really feel I want to fall in love, and I might even fall in love a little, a little. But then when I get back to the city I'll avoid that woman for three or four weeks. I'll use these other people's attractiveness as an antidote against the attraction I might feel for the lady." He laughed and looked out the window. His face was handsome when he faced you, but in profile he looked a slight bit mousy. This was because he had a receding chin. Outside the window, Fiftieth Street was crowded. A bus pulled to the curb to pick up passengers. Two older women got on. For the time being, the bus blocked the view of the street. Then it pulled away, blowing black smoke from underneath.

"I'll think about her, and I'll smile when I think of the good times we had, but I won't call. You might call it running from her," he said. "Have fun with me. Enjoy me, but don't try to get too close. It bothers me," he said, overloud, and laughed.

"Then, you like it that way?" I asked.

"Yeah, I have a good life."

"You ever sit down and figure out why you're like that?"

"No." He looked back out the dirty window. "I just accept that about myself. I like to play the field; different women have different attractions. I used to think it was something about my past, but it doesn't have to be that. It could just be a matter of the way certain people are made up. I used to say it was because of things that happened to me when I was a little kid.

"I was born on the east side of Baltimore, in the ghetto, man. Right in the middle, and a lot of shit hurt me very bad. I can't always remember specific hurts, but I know I was hurt very often as a child—being poor, not having things. Not even having enough to eat sometimes.

"My father worked himself to death at menial jobs. My mother worked her life away in someone else's kitchen. I was very sensitive to this while it was happening to me. I felt sorry for them, and I didn't want anything like that to happen to me.

"You know, sometimes I used to lay in bed and cry about what I felt life had in store for me, and cry about what my parents and the grown people around me had to suffer. I mean about my father, working for people who disrespected him, as a longshoreman, a truck driver, a handyman—always at some menial job which he was always losing, until in the end it got to be his fault. He was so hostile toward the end that I could understand why he lost his jobs. But it wasn't his fault that he was like that in the first place. I mean, I'm sure that once he was a very good cat. One thing, he never was mean to me or my mother, but he would take these long walks rather than risk exploding around us. He was just not a cruel cat, and I remember one time he hit my mother and he cried more than she did.

"She kept telling him that it was all right. That she wasn't hurt, and he just cried and cried and she couldn't make him stop crying. I remember that. I ran and hid behind the bed, and then he came and got me, and he was still crying and saying he was sorry. This was a very terrible thing in my life. I felt so sorry for him. But this is all very confusing to an eight-year-old boy.

"You know what frightened me most about that? It frightened me because I knew that me and my father were just alike, so in a way what I've done is try to change me, but when I realize I can't change, I avoid situations.

"I'm like that now. I cry now in movies and stuff. I don't know why. I cry when I'm with someone I could love. I'll just be talking and we'll be communicating so beautiful and I'll feel so good that I'll just start crying—but then that's the person I avoid, because I know that she's gotten close to me and I don't want that.

"But I don't know. I tell myself that I avoid all the shit that my parents went through, but maybe that isn't the reason. Sometimes I think I avoid love because I'm afraid of being rejected. I reject other people before they have a chance to reject me.

"Maybe the thing is that at twenty-seven years old I'm beginning to accept the fact that I'm a timid person—emotionally timid. Maybe I've always been. One proof that I'm not avoiding love to make a lot of money is that I don't make a lot of money. I make fifteen thousand dollars a year. That wouldn't qualify me as a hard-nosed, loveless robber baron, would it?" he laughed. We looked out the window for a while and worked on our sandwiches. The steak was tender. I ordered coffee.

"I do read all those books about money, though: *The Rich and the Super Rich, David Rockefeller, Supermoney*. If I take a book away with me on a weekend, it'll be a book like that. That's the only kind of book that holds my interest, the only kind that has enough excitement," he said.

For the first time, I noticed that Billy did not have a mustache, like most young black men. He looked younger than twenty-seven and very easygoing. I thought about all the women who told me they were looking for a gentle black man. Many black women said black men are always trying to prove their masculinity. They're very seldom gentle. I remember one young woman in particular who had lived in the Caribbean with a Frenchman for four months. She admitted that she didn't love him, "But he was the gentlest man I've ever been involved with," the girl said. "His ego was so much intact that he didn't always have to be proving his manhood. I get so tired of the ego games that black men think they have to play."

Billy Fowler made me think about the black men who say, conversely, that "A black woman can't love a man who doesn't express his manhood in very physical ways. She doesn't want a man who isn't rough. Subconsciously, she wants to be dominated."

"Gentleness is one of those things that black women need but can accept from other men more easily than they can accept it from their own," someone way back had said. Maybe they know too much about what the world has done to very gentle black men.

"So I guess timid would be it," Billy said. "I think of myself as being too vulnerable emotionally to be successful in the business of life, unless I keep people at a distance." He ordered coffee.

"I think I could marry a woman I didn't love," he said. "I think I would rather marry a woman I liked rather than one I loved. I think fun is better than love. I didn't have a lot of fun as a kid. I think success is better than love. When you look at it, man, love is not all that great," he laughed. His coffee came.

"For example, last year I took this girl to Bermuda over the Easter weekend. It was really nice. I was *so* happy, man. She's a beautiful girl—lives up in the Bronx, has a black mother and East Indian father from Trinidad. We had a very nice time. I could have fallen in love if I had let myself go. We fit together well. We'd make love and both of us would be completely satisfied at the same time, and then we'd fall asleep together. We were compatible in all forms.

"Then, when I got back to the States, I didn't want to see her for about three months. She left messages for me but I never returned her calls. When she finally did get together with me, she asked, 'Where you been?' I said, 'Busy making money,'" he laughed. "I have this unconscious desire to be rich and powerful. What makes me laugh is that I only have five hundred dollars in my savings account, and I have thousands of dollars in debts to Master Charge, BankAmericard, TWA Getaway Card for all these nice trips.

"I make enough to pay my monthly bills, but in savings I've only got five hundred dollars. I don't know." He laughed again. He was a pleasant man. "I'd like to read that book; I'd like to know about how other people relate to each other. You always want to know how much you're missing, if anything. A book like that I could take away with me on a trip and just dig on the way other people handle their lives." He had long since finished his sandwich. I was still a little hungry but he said, "Hey, man, I got to get back. I got to jump and run. Anyway, I told you all I know about love from my own private point of view, but I know some sisters you ought to talk to."

He gave me some names while we walked to the counter to pay the check. Outside, the weather was hot. "Love is really a messed-up thing. So I really haven't let myself be in love with anybody. I think black people are too emotional, anyway," he said. We watched the prostitutes on Fiftieth Street hanging out waiting for noon hour business. "We're too emotional to live in a capitalistic society. While we're worrying about emotional shit, other people are out making money.

"I got this theory, man: If the African brothers who sold us into slavery had come over here, they woulda done better financially than we have. They had the knack for making money. You can tell that by the fact we're the ones who got sold. The other brothers must have had that agressive, acquisitive mentality that's lacking in so many people I know." We crossed Seventh Avenue. "I work at night now, so I go to school during the day and I take this course in graduate economics, and while the teacher's explaining, lecturing, I'm sitting there daydreaming about these economic theories that explain things. Like that one that explains why black people do so poorly economically in this country. Can you dig it?"

"I have to think about it for a while."

"Check it out." We walked slowly, because we were coming to his building and I could tell that he was not finished rapping. "Check it out. Love is beautiful but it's non-functional, man. So I've been transforming myself, making myself over into a single-minded, aggressive, acquisitive sort of person." He laughed at himself. "I went to college with the white bourgeoisie. I learned a lot from them. Their ideas on love are different. I began seeing the advantages in all that pragmatic, high-church-type non-emotionalism.

"Shit, I been thinking about joining the Episcopal Church myself." He laughed and started to go inside the building where his class is. I wondered how much of what he said was serious and how much was a joke at his own expense. "Check it out: Lutheranism, Anglicanism, Episcopalianism . . . ," he said, holding the door open.

"Poor people, black and white, are the ones who worry about a lot of emotional shit. Rich people equate love with other things, like money, like Jackie Onassis," he laughed.

"So if you say love to me, I'd say it ain't nothing deep, nothing deep enough to get in my way. It ain't no heavy thing. It can be controlled. I want to be like that. I want to be a wealthy, high-church Republican," he said and laughed.

13

Jimmy Bennet

Your father didn't love your mother.
Is that why you can't love me?

James Bennet lives alone on the first floor of a $410,000 brownstone between Park and Madison avenues just north of Fifty-seventh Street. The streets are quiet in this section of Manhattan, where few black people and no poor people can afford to live.

"Hey! Come in," he said. "Grab a seat." He is dark-skinned. A handsome man. At six foot two, he is taller than I am; at thirty-two, he was a year younger. He owns his own real estate firm and pays himself around $60,000 a year. He was, I suspected, the only millionaire I'd get to interview.

"How you doing?" I asked. He got me inside his house and we exchanged small talk.

"You drink scotch?" he asked.

"Sure." I had been drinking wine all day in the Village, but I knew he would have good scotch. I didn't mind changing to something soft like Chivas Regal, which is what he had, judging from the elegance of everything else. The furniture was modern, the oval table top of expensive glass rested delicately on a pedestal that curved and twisted like natural driftwood.

I sat down in a chair of white leather across from a set of stereo components that were tied into a giant-screen TV. Above this were two paintings. Both were abstract. One was reddish like a bleeding landscape, the other bluish like a crying cityscape. It was not the Manhattan skyline, but it was similar. It was an expensive room of white and burgundy. James Bennet looked a little out of place in it. He was not as well tailored as the room. His mustache was a little crooked. His Afro had the frizzies.

"So Linda Wilson told me you were doing a book on love," he said. He was behind the white bar, fixing drinks.

"Yeah, she said you were a lover."

"Who? me? Naw," he laughed. I decided that his accent was a little southern. "She didn't say that. Not about me." He laughed again. "I think that's a good idea, though. If I saw a book on love—the way black people love—I would buy it. You know why?"

"Why?" I sat way back in the deep leather armchair.

"I got my own theories about it, man, and I think a lot of

other people think like I do. I would buy the book for that reason. Love is nice, man, but I've only been in love once in my life. That was with this girl named Gloria Amos, ten years ago, in my hometown, East St. Louis, Illinois. She's the only woman I can say I ever really loved."

I put my tape recorder down softly on the glass-topped table. We exchanged more small talk, but not much. I relaxed and he relaxed. I felt good because I was sure the interview was going to be easy. James Bennet acted like a man who liked to get done whatever he came to do.

"I've been with other women, and for some of them I've felt a great deal—like Linda, for example. I liked her very much," he said. "But I've never loved anybody else. Only once was I ever in love. That's why I would read the book, because I have this theory. Linda and I were talking about it the night she asked me about you coming to interview. I was telling her I think most people fall in love only once. One time." He gulped a little of his drink. "Once," he said and held up one finger, as I had seen someone else do for the same reason. He gave me my scotch and sat down on the burgundy footstool instead of the deep burgundy hopsack chair. He leaned forward. He seemed to be a very intense man.

"I was in love for two years, the last two years of high school, so in a way you could say that she was my high school sweetheart, but it was more than just a high school thing. It was actually the strongest feelings I've ever had for another human being," he said. He took a sip of scotch, swished it around in his mouth, and then swallowed.

"That would be my theory, that by the time you're over twenty-one or twenty-two you've been fucked around so much by life that you really can't love anybody any more—not in the same way, not the way you did when you were in your foolish teens.

"Back then, that was love. This bullshit that you feel now— I mean, it was strong then. It was so strong that it would scare you. It could make you get cold in July and hot in December. It could make you dizzy. Remember? You couldn't even pee straight, your dick'd be so hard. You remember how your stomach would knot up and you'd feel so good you'd actually hurt? Your body would hurt. That was love. You didn't hold back. You put everything in it.

"I admit that right now I wish I could love another human being that much, but I know I'll never love that way again. See, one reason I remember the feeling so well is that Gloria Amos was in New York about three months ago—February; no, March." He crossed his legs and rested his weight on his elbows on the seat of the chair. His socks were as smooth and dark as his face—a face so smooth that he seemed never to have shaved. There were no razor bumps. His Afro started far back on his smooth forehead.

Leaning back in the dim light, he seemed to belong to no particular occupation. He had not taken on the appearance of any particular occupational group: businessman, athlete, teacher. None of them and all of them could easily fit. His eyes said that there was something that he worked very hard at. He said he never got more than four or five hours sleep a night. He said he didn't need more than that. His eyes said he did. They were yellowish and a little bloodshot.

I asked him if he had a picture of her. He said not. I asked him what she looked like.

He said, "She's a big woman. I like big women. I like to be able to feel something when I hold a woman." He leaned forward and cupped his hands in front of him to show how he liked to hold a woman. "She's light-skinned. Tall.

"I loved her because I was absolutely sure she loved me for me, for the person I am. That's the only way it can be. A person has to love you for this. . . ." He pointed to his heart and his head, then he cupped his hands and shook them in front of himself to indicate the rest of himself. "Me. If it's not for that, it's not for real. And here in March when I saw her I knew she still loved me, and I loved her. You never really stop loving someone like that.

"So when I saw her I hurt and felt good at the same time. You know how you sometimes hurt and feel good all at once. She looked good, man. She looked damn good," he laughed.

I put my scotch on the table where the tape recorder was.

Linda Wilson had told me that James Bennet was worth a million dollars. She was in a position to know. She had worked for him and had lived with him for a while. She said he had come as close as he could to loving her, but in the end he couldn't love, and she couldn't settle for anything less than that. They'd drifted apart.

"Things happen to me gradually, man. I wouldn't tell you anything about myself to make my life seem like an endless trauma. I've never had a trauma. I don't have traumas. Right now, the impact of it hits me more than it did when it was happening, way back then.

"The impact of love, thinking back on it. I miss it. I remember that I took her to the senior prom on a bus. That's how poor we were. I can imagine how we must have looked going to the prom on a bus—floor-length, baby-blue gown, white, semiformal rented coat on the bus in the middle of the night, sober. I didn't drink in those days.

"I think about it now, but I didn't think that much about it then. That must have been funny. Gloria and I were laughing about it when we were together in March. That was the first time I'd seen her since she got married," he said. I asked him again if he had said that she was married now.

"I'm not ashamed of that. She didn't ditch me to marry this guy. As I said, it was a matter of a few years between me and him. Gloria and I drifted apart when I went into the Army, ten years ago. She's only been married to this guy about five years. She didn't run out on me or nothing. I haven't been fucked up, these last few years, thinking about this woman who ran out on me. That doesn't explain why I haven't loved anyone else. That doesn't explain it. I guess the explanation is that I just haven't had the urge to love anyone else," he said.

"For one thing, I don't think it's easy for me to love a person. This has something to do with my background. There are very few people in my background, but most of those people are males. The males have played a dominant role, my grandfather being the most dominant. And the biggest thing that this old man taught me is that a man should be in control of his emotions at all times. At all times." He was now sitting in the burgundy easy chair. His glass of scotch was beside him on the floor. He leaned back farther out of the light from the lamp.

"If you say that black people are usually very emotional, that's true. I'm just the opposite, though. With me it started with the emotion of fear. My grandfather made me control my fear, because in his work he had to leave me at home for weeks at a time by myself. I was only five or six and I had to stay in the house for weeks by myself.

"He was a traveling salesman for funeral-home supplies all over Missouri, Arkansas, and Tennessee. He had to be gone a lot, so he would never let me show him that I was afraid to stay home by myself.

"I was afraid, though. We lived in one of those isolated shacks that you see along the roadside all through the South; you know, the kind that sits up off the ground because the ground floods about once a year. Me and him lived alone in one of those.

"Out in front was the main highway, so that was cool. Cars and trucks were always coming along, but out back there was nothing, man. Nothing but empty fields. Then there was a row of trees and then the river. That was the only thing outside my bedroom window at night: the empty fields and the fucking river.

"You have to remember that this started when I was five years old. I used to lay in there at night by myself. I used to think that anything could come across those fields and get me. But my grandfather wouldn't let me tell him that I was afraid. He'd say, 'Boy, you ain't scared. Ain't nothing gonna bother you.' That's the way he talked. And he'd go off. I was there by myself. I cooked for myself and put myself out to school. I did it all, me for me.

"So in time I learned to control every facet of my emotional expression. I learned to control myself in all respects, and that has nothing at all to do with being cool, or supercool, as they say, or the life-style of a pimp. Those are kids' games. My life has nothing to do with that.

"I dress well and I live well, but I would never play at

being cool. With me it's just a matter of not showing much emotion. Gloria, by contrast, is a very emotional person, very sensitive. I guess that's the main reason why we ain't together today. She always gave her emotions to me freely, but I couldn't give mine back to her. I wanted to. I loved her, but I didn't let love pour out like she did. In fact, I'll tell you how I am. This is the kind of person I am. Sometimes I was actually ashamed of the emotions I did feel for her," he said and laughed slightly. Then he asked me if I needed another drink.

I said yes. "Then, are you cool?" I asked, joking.

"No. Instead I'm a very warm person in my way, but only in my way." He got up to fix two more drinks.

"There's a black woman psychologist from Howard University who says that black people can't love," I said as he moved from behind the bar.

"I don't know, man. I don't think about it that much. Gloria is black. She loves. Black people are very affectionate, emotional people."

"But not you?"

"No. I know what the psychologist might be trying to say. As a kid I didn't see women giving love to men or men giving love to women. I never saw that. It's not in my experience. It's not in my background. I saw men dancing with women like they wanted to grind a hole in them. I saw people joking, but I didn't see affectionate touching.

"People are strange. People are a trip. I lived with one of my uncles once. I saw him and my aunt fighting, but I never saw them touching in love. They would fight right out in front of my face, but when they made love they would go and hide." He laughed. His face came forward into the light. He picked up his scotch and took a sip.

"But I'm not saying that any of this is the whole reason why I'm not an affectionate person. I don't blame any of it on that. I just think that this is the way I am. Obviously." He sat back again. "I don't think I'm a bitter person, but I do think that Gloria did the best thing by going and marrying another-type person."

"I don't believe that," I said.

"It's up to you to believe what you want to believe. I think she did the right thing. I miss her, but I'm not the kind of person who has a lot of regrets about the past. I don't think about the past much.

"For example, I haven't been back to East St. Louis but once in the last seven years. I went back in the spring of 1969, to my grandfather's funeral. It was a strange thing. He had a fairly large funeral, but almost everyone there was male. I don't mean by that that my grandfather was a homo or something like that. He was jamming women up into his sixties. It's just that he had a very male-oriented life. He had all sons, no daughters, and no wife.

"At the funeral was the first time I saw my father in my adult life. He's a good-looking, young-looking dude, considering he must be well into his fifties. He lives pretty good, in Oakland, California. I was actually born in Oakland, but I know very little about the California part of my life. My mother died when I was about three, and my father sent me to East St. Louis to live with his father.

"My old man is tall and dark-skinned, like me. I look a lot like him. He's heavier than I am, but he's slim for a fifty-year-old man. I met him at Crawford's Funeral Home, by accident more or less. He was staying with one of his brothers in St. Louis, and we both had come to the funeral home at the same time to view the body. We were glad to see each other. He seemed to be doing okay. I guess both of us were glad that the other one wasn't a bum.

"What happens to a lot of cats after they start making pretty good money is that their long-lost relatives start showing up asking for money. I'm glad my father wasn't a bum like that. He seemed to be doing okay. I'm glad he didn't ask me for money. He didn't ask to get involved with my life either, and he didn't ask me to get involved with his. He didn't leave me his telephone number, and he didn't ask for mine.

"You might not believe it, but I was glad he didn't, and I was proud of him for not trying to say that he was sorry that he hadn't kept in touch all these years. I liked him a whole lot because of that. That way, we both could look each other in the eye and not have to look away." James Bennet laughed, thinking that he had wandered away from the subject. He brought himself back.

"So I guess all of this had to do with the way I see love, man. I was different from Gloria. Like she said when she was here, 'The thing I enjoy is kissing my family,' she said, 'Kissing my husband when he leaves for work in the morning. Kissing my children when they go off to school. Then I go and teach my seventh grade, and I'm home in time to kiss them when they get home.'

"I said, 'That's nice.' She knew I never did like a lot of touching. I touch only under the most intimate circumstances. Otherwise I tend to keep my hands to myself. I don't relish physical contact. The casual brushing and touching of people is something I avoid.

"Gloria and I were sitting in the bedroom here talking about this, drinking. She was sitting just swinging her big, pretty legs. She was laughing a lot. She laughs a lot when she's drinking. She can't drink much still. She never could. She doesn't know how to drink. She's a wife, man. She's not a party girl, she's just one of these big old pretty wives. You're right, I regretted that I didn't marry her, but we're so different and I respect that difference.

"I don't get offended if people aren't always laying their hands on me. I like it that way. I've seen people get hurt close up, my uncles and their wives and women. I've seen people really get hurt close up. People who were close to me. I felt sorry for them when they got hurt and I don't like feeling sorry. Feeling sorry for people is a very uncomfortable thing for me."

"Do you consider that a hang-up?"

"Naw, man; I function."

"I guess everyone is hung up to an extent," I said.

"I think you're only hung up if you can't function, if you need some kind of freaky shit to get you over. I'm all right. I like myself. You can tell that I approve of myself by my life-style—by the food I eat and the way I dress—and I don't mean mod dressing or dressing like a hustler.

"That's a very destructive image, that image of the ba-a-ad

black motherfucka. I don't try to be a hard, urban mother-fucka. I see a lot of those young black kids around the corner at that disco, The Martinique, trying so hard to walk like a pimp and talk like a pimp and treat their girls as a pimp would treat a girl. I date a lot of girls only to keep from dating one girl.

"I've never wanted to be a pimp. I got too much respect for the rights of others. I've never wanted to be a bad mother-fucka with chicks lined up supporting me. I work hard for what I get and I'm generous with that. I'd rather give a woman something than to take something from her.

"To me, a pimp is a weak person. I've never hit a woman in my life, man. You know that? I've never hit a woman. I'm actually a very generous cat. I share with people—my money, you can borrow anything I got if you think you need it. You can borrow material things, but you can't borrow too much of me. If you come to me and say, 'Jimmy, how about running me down the Village?' I'd say, 'Here, you take my car.' I don't know why I'm like that. One of my New Year's resolutions was to be more selfish with my thirteen-thousand-dollar Mercedes and less selfish with myself."

"Yeah, it is easy to share things," I said. "It's harder to share you."

"I know that. You're not telling me anything new by pointing that out. When you've said that, you haven't said shit that I don't already know. I compensate for, or overcompensate for it in the work area. I work and don't think about it.

"So if you'd judge my life comparatively, you'd have to say I live a pretty good life. I travel a lot and I do the things I want to do. I was in Jamaica last Christmas. I was in Acapulco before that. I'm not money-hungry, but money does mean that I don't have to work for petty people. You can work for people who make you hate yourself for having to work for them. I don't have to subject myself to other people's whims. If I had grown up without an education, I would've robbed a bank before I'd've worked for some bastard down in the garment district or somewhere. I could kill somebody before I would do that all my life.

"If it put me in an emotionally uncomfortable position I

think I could take a motherfucka off. But as it so happened I was able to make good money. When I got out of the Army I had saved two thousand dollars. I went to Chicago, and me and a guy named Jerome Powell started setting up laundromats all over the South Side. Every time we'd get one going good, we'd set up another one. I lived that shit for two solid years of my life, two years. I installed most of the shit myself with one helper out of the back end of a 1957 Chevy van truck—in winter, summer. I worked my ass off.

"After two years, we had seventeen of them. You'd be surprised how much money there is in laundromats, how fast the money grows with those nickels, dimes, and quarters rolling in every day, sixteen hours a day, out of hundreds of machines.

"Then I got into real estate. I bought a broken-down car wash, fixed it up, and sold it five months later for twenty-eight thousand dollars more than I paid for it. I knew how to make money turn over. I was a welder in the Army and I took a couple of business-school courses at night.

"Two months before I turned twenty-eight, I sold out to Jerome Powell and went into business for myself. I would buy houses in neighborhoods where other people wouldn't buy, but I didn't run no slumlord shit. I didn't have to. I could judge people, where the average white landlord couldn't, or didn't want to. I rented to people who would keep a place up if I fixed it up, and I fixed up every place I bought. I turned the money over. I turned it over.

"But I certainly didn't plan my life as a money-maker. As a kid I didn't lay awake dreaming about making money. I still don't think of myself as an overly ambitious person. I'm not compulsive. I simply respond to what feels comfortable to me.

"I was a dude who could travel in a straight line from an uncomfortable situation to one that was more comfortable. Money is neither the cause of me nor the reason for me. That's why I use money so well. It doesn't use me. I don't sit on it like a miser. I force it to treat me well.

"I'm like a tree, man. I grow toward the sun. If I'd've been emotionally more comfortable in a situation that would've produced less money, then I'd still be the same person I am. I loved. I loved as much as anyone else has down here on this motherfucka. It's just that all my life I've been suspicious of a lot of kissing and hugging. It all seems like so much protocol without any true meaning. I'm not completely a cold person. Women don't find me cold, but I do have this tendency to close down quickly if something doesn't feel right emotionally.

"When my grandfather died, I closed down. He meant a great deal to me, but I couldn't see any reason to cry after he was dead. He was a very decent human being, and I would say I loved him very much, but I went to his funeral and didn't cry. If I had cried, that would've been nothing but a public show, protocol, like so much of this hugging and kissing that you see at airports.

"If people want me to feel sorry for them, I'm not going to do that. They can go off and feel sorry by themselves, but then, when they come back and they're ready to fight the thing that made them sad, then they'll find other people closing down and me opening up. A million people will feel sorry for you, but when you're ready to fight, where will they be?

"I act out love, man. I don't sit around and talk about it. Gloria loved me. She admitted that she missed me and that she may have made a mistake, but I was the one who went off to the Army and didn't tell her what I was going to do.

"I'm not saying that she's unhappy. She's happily married. I asked her when she was here if she's ever made love to another man since she's been married. She said she had—to one man.

"'My husband's affectionate without being particularly sexual,' she said. 'So I've been tempted, and I yielded to temptation with one man on about a half dozen occasions.'

"I laughed when she said that, because she always accused me of being sexual without being affectionate. So you see, you never get exactly what you want.

"I made love to her. I was the second outside dude she had been to bed with since she got married. She missed me. She said she missed me because for the space of four years, from eighteen to twenty-two, I was between her thighs every time I could get her panties down—on the bed, on the floor, under the porch with cars coming by, on the porch in the swing, in the fields—I used to jam her. I loved her.

"I don't even tell a woman now that I'm in love. I won't lie about that. But, one day . . . I may be incapable of falling in love, but if I'm not I'd like to fall in love. I'd like to fall in love because I want to have children—a little boy—and I would never have a child if I wasn't married, and I wouldn't marry unless I'm really in love.

"Most of all, man, I want to be reasonably sure that the marriage will work out. I think it's only natural for a kid to have two parents who honestly love and respect each other. I think that's very natural. What's unnatural is for a kid to grow up without two parents. That's the way I grew up."

14

Nothing Better in the Universe

There're still a lot of old-fashioned women in New York–
I'm one of them.

"I think I put a lot into a love affair because as a child I grew up wanting only that: a relationship with a good man and children. So even though I've had some bad experiences with men, I haven't let them turn me bitter. I still very much believe in love," Selinda said. She is a small woman. We are in her kitchen, because that's where she likes to spend her time. It is clean and comfortable here. I get up from a chair at the table and go to the window.

Outside, children are using the hot, littered street as a playground. An abandoned car sits in front of the building. The children climb on it. I watch them while I listen.

"People sometimes ask me why I'm not more bitter after some of the things that've happened to me. I feel I'm not because I don't think of life in terms of what a man did to me. I try to understand what was inside him to make him do whatever it was he did.

"I have a tendency to try and understand things from the other person's point of view. Most women don't realize that a black man's life is nothing but problems, and this might make him somewhat callous to your problems. Some men have so many problems that they don't want to hear that you've got problems too." From across the room she looks smaller than she had before. Her Afro seems to frame a smaller face. She seems almost petite. Serious.

"I can understand that, but I'm glad that that's not the way my man is." Her man is her husband and the father of the youngest of her two children. He is away working. "Some women, some women I know, will run over a very gentle man. They need a man who's aggressive and always showing his masculinity by fighting. They need a man who likes to curse all the time and is very physical. I don't need that. Joe is very gentle.

"The society hasn't allowed many black men to grow up gentle," she said. "Take both my brothers. They lived very short, unhappy lives, and they died violently." She took the coffeepot off the fire. "I raised both of them and I learned a lot about men from them. They were younger than I was but they grew up faster, and so I used to listen to the problem they had with women. From them I learned that a black man doesn't need a woman always fussing and nagging. I tuned in to them, and that oriented me to the way I deal with a man," she said. I stayed at the window and looked out at the low, drab skyline of the Southeast Bronx. The sky above it, clean, blue, contained a sun of pleasant intensity. The heat of the day seemed to come from the earth itself.

"My brothers, they were like a lot of black men; a lot of black men have not experienced being cuddled when they were babies. They had very little tenderness in their lives when they were young. And that's very important." She got sugar down. I still hadn't decided if she was petite or not, but she stood on tiptoe to get sugar off the second shelf. "But you take the men who grew up down South. They're different from northern children. They received more love. If they didn't get love from their mothers, they got it from an aunt, they got it from a grandmother, they got it from the old woman next door; they got it. You find that they're much warmer than northern people." She stood there by the counter with her faded jeans hugging her hips tightly. They were the kind of jeans that flared at the bottom and laced in the back.

"My brothers didn't have that mother love before they died. My mother worked full time, so I raised five brothers and sisters. Sometimes you have a child who doesn't care that his mother has to go to work. He doesn't get affected by the fact that his sister has to raise him, but then there's always *one* child, one child who needs his mother. Not that I didn't do the best I could to raise them; I did the best I could, but how can you cuddle someone who's only three years younger than yourself?" she asked. I didn't know. She didn't either, and she laughed in the way people laugh when they have used an unanswerable question and laughter to show that most of life is unanswerable.

"So one of my brothers was shot by a cop when I was pregnant with my daughter. That was a traumatic experience for me, because he had just gotten out of jail that August." She got milk from the refrigerator. It was condensed milk in a small can with the Borden's cow on front.

"What happened was he had been beaten up by a policeman down on Forty-second Street. So we went to court to press charges against the policeman. We took him down to Center Street to press charges against the policeman who had beaten him up, and there were other policemen there who accused him of conspiracy to rob. We took him down and he never even got to come home. They put him in jail. They brought him to trial and gave him two years on Rikers Island." She had been standing with the refrigerator door open, thinking, remembering. She is slightly taller than the door.

"He got out of jail that August and he was dead by September. A policeman shot him down on 126th Street. They said they told him to put up his hands and he made a funny motion and they shot him. Nothing was done about it. So much stuff about the black man has been swept under the rug." She laughed again in that same way.

"I was five months pregnant then and I wasn't married, so my brother and I had been close. We used to talk all the time. He used to say how he was going to take the baby to the park, or take him to play ball, or what not. I think he wanted me to have that baby more than I did.

"I was very hurt about what happened to him and about the way it happened, and the way it was hushed up. So I have very tender feelings for the black man, because he has been oppressed more than the black woman. That's why when I hear about women's liberation it doesn't faze me. I laugh.

"That's why I can't say nothing against this very cold, hard black man. I know he's out there. Yes, there're some very bitter men out there. But if they're bitter, they have a right to be," she said. "But because of my nature I need a sensitive man. I've always been very sensitive. When I was a child if you looked at me wrong, I'd cry. Sometimes I think I'm too sensitive, because the world's a very hard place to deal with.

"But then there are times when I'm glad I am like I am. When my man looks at me in a certain way I can tune in to him. I know when something is wrong with him; and if I come to him in a certain way, he knows that I have a problem. At those times I'm glad I'm sensitive." Down in the street kids were still crawling through a hole in the shattered windshield of the abandoned car. I wondered if her children were down there, but I didn't ask. I liked listening to her. I moved from the window back to the kitchen table, where she had put a cup of coffee. She held hers in both hands, cup in one hand and saucer in the other. She used her chin to wipe a drop of coffee off the outside of the cup.

"The first thing I notice about a man is his hands. You can look at a man's hands and tell if he would be gentle, or if he's sure of himself, or whatever. Then I look at his eyes. Then, I like a bowlegged man. Bowlegged men turn me on. So, in a way, I got what I want. Joe is a little bowlegged," she laughed. "I'm very much in love. Yes, I'll tell anybody that.

"But I don't think you should talk up your man too much. Many women are just waiting for you to blow your good man," she said. "Curiosity is a powerful thing. You'll tell your girl friend how good your man is and she begins to say to herself, 'Hm, I better check this out!' And nine times out of ten she'll go after your man and get him, because a man is basically a roamer. For him there's nothing like a new thing.

"All men run around," she said. This was an amazing bit of acceptance for a woman who had described herself as very jealous. But most black women I talked to agreed with her: "All men run around." Marriage was a pair of shoes that didn't seem to fit a race of men with big feet, corns, bunions; who had been forced by circumstances to go barefoot for so long. Only a few men could wear them at all.

"But some men have their thing so under control that they don't let their wives know about it. They have respect for their marriage. They don't have their outside women calling the house." She pointed to the wall telephone above her chair. "They don't come home late at night smelling like another woman."

"They come home smelling like soap," I said.

"Yeah," she laughed, pointed to me, and rolled her eyes. "They don't empty their pocket on the dresser and have another woman's telephone number balled up on a piece of paper. They're cool with it. That's all a woman wants. Just be cool; just don't let me know. What else you do to satisfy yourself, keep it separate from your marriage," she said. She is stern. She is teaching.

"Very seldom will you find a man who hasn't got someone on the outside that he's dealing with on some level. A man who's been hurt once will never put all his eggs in one basket. That's right. He goes into his next relationship expecting to be hurt, so he keeps someone on the outside to fall back on, because he expects to be eventually put down.

"And then, women are such beautiful things to a man. They are creatures, creatures of different moods and experiences, and a man never gets tired of checking them out to see how this one is or that one is. He can't help it. That's his nature." Her mouth was full of these words. She savored them.

"Most women are not like that. Most women stick to one man, and if it's not working out, they hang onto that man and slowly ease into another man. I think a woman conditions herself to a man—to his habits and his likes and dislikes, so if you have a man who you're used to, who is satisfying you physically, spiritually, and mentally, you will stick with that man, and you won't take the chance of blowing your good man just for a one-night stand."

"You really believe that? Most women don't run around?" I asked.

"Sometimes, but not as much, because a woman will forgive a man for running around; very seldom will you find a man who'll forgive a woman for that.

"Men have the souls of roamers. Their needs are more intense. A woman's nature is different. They need emotional security. They need to trust a man before they can really love him. When a woman runs around, it's because she's been hurt and she's afraid to trust. She has a tendency to say, 'I've been hurt by one man, so I'm not going to put myself in a position to be hurt again.' She goes into an affair superficially. She extends herself so far, but then she's ready to draw back. She plays games with her feelings and with the feelings of the man she's dealing with.

Nothing Better in the Universe   193

"I don't like to hold back. I've been hurt, but basically if I hold back I'm only hurting myself. I can't hold back. There were times when I wouldn't deal with men at all, because I knew I wasn't ready to put myself completely into a love affair. Even when I was young I was like that: all or nothing." She finally sat down. Her movements said she was restless.

Her calm voice suggested that she was cooled out. "I was married before, when I was eighteen. I was married for a little while when I was eighteen, and even though it was a disaster from the start, I tried to understand things from my husband's point of view. We never did really live together. After we got married he decided that he wanted to live with his mother. So I said, 'Okay, if that's what you want.' He was a very dependent individual and it began to bother me. How would you like it if, every day, a man was telling you, 'My mother didn't do it this way, or my mother didn't do it that way, or my mother did it this way'?

"The marriage was annulled after eleven months, but I wasn't angry with him until about a year and a half later. I was in the hospital having my daughter, and he came and told the nurse that he was my husband and that prevented my man from coming to see the baby; that's the first time I got mad at him." She laughed.

"This man who wanted to see you in the hospital—were you in love with him, too?"

"Very much. Whenever I've been in love it's been very, very much. I loved this man, but things ended badly with him. He had a lot of dog in his nature."

"Dog?"

"Yes, dog." She didn't stutter, stammer, or explain. "I'd been going with him for a long time and one day he came to me and told me he didn't love me any more, that he loved Cicely, my friend. I was very hurt, because our relationship had been very happy, so I thought. I had moved up in the Bronx so I could be near him. We couldn't live together because I had a daughter and I didn't want to live with a man without being married, because that would be a bad example for my daughter.

"But we saw each other almost every day. I was hurt most because I felt I had put everything into that relationship. I was shocked, because it came without warning. We didn't have an argument. He came over and said that he didn't dig me any more. He dug Cicely, my friend. He had some jazz albums over my house and he picked up those and that was all there was to it.

"What I learned from that is never talk your man up around another woman. I was all the time telling Cicely how ba-a-a-ad my man was and how he could do this and do that. How he could make your toes curl up and your scalp itch and goose-pimples break out and your eyeballs roll back in your head when he touched you. I used to tell her that it seemed like he never got tired, and so quite naturally she said, 'Hm, I better go and check this out.' And she did. So he went with her.

"I'm not the kind to fight, though. I loved him, but if you stop digging someone, you shouldn't stay together and fight or hold malice, or take that bitterness into your next relationship. You should leave. Which is what he did.

"He started living with Cicely. They stayed together for a few months and then they broke up. He wanted us to get back together but I was already dealing with Joe. He said he felt he had made a mistake, but I feel like this: If I put everything into a relationship and you decide that you don't want it, then you had to do a lot of thinking about it to come to that conclusion. You had to toy with it inside yourself for a long while to come to that conclusion. I don't think it was a mistake. I think it was a particular time in your life and you saw something else you thought you wanted.

"After he got with Cicely, though, he found out that I had spoiled him. That's why in some ways it's not good to be too good to a man. If something happens and the two of you can't make it, you've already conditioned him to having a woman taking care of all his needs. Then he gets with another woman, who's not going to do all that, and he goes through something like withdrawal symptoms. I never hassle a man.

Nothing Better in the Universe   195

There's never no money hassle, never no clothes hassle, and most women out there are not like that," she said. I listened.

I had never heard that line of thinking from a woman so young. I had heard it from an older woman in my father's church over twenty years ago. The woman had gotten up in church to testify and had started by shouting, "I can't die now, Lord. Who's gonna take care of Wilbur? Nobody, Lord, knows how Wilbur likes his eggs, Jesus"; she threw up her arms and shouted, "Nobody knows how to fix his tea and that he likes his fried chicken crisp, Lord, and nobody knows that but me." She moaned and the church trembled. "Oh, Jesus, Jesus, Jesus. I don't want to come home now."

"I'm that way basically because of my mother," Selinda said. "A whole lot of her came out in me," she laughed. "She's been married thirty years and she's still very much in love, and that's amazing if you consider all that that woman has been through. We talk all the time, and she'll tell me in a minute that she loves her husband. I remember, when we were young, she was always cheerful. She never woke up with an attitude. She was always calm. My father would be walking around the house yelling and throwing things. She would just say, 'Okay, Walter, I hear you!' She's a beautiful woman. I used to ask her why didn't she leave him. I couldn't stay with a man who was always yelling. She'd say, 'But I love him.' I'd say, 'Well said, Moms,'" she laughed.

She was leaning across the green kitchen table with her hands wrapped around her coffee cup. Her fingers were small. One of them contained a small diamond wedding ring. Sitting down, she didn't look as small. She was a well-proportioned woman. I thought of how lucky her husband was. She was both big and small. She could be a tree or a flower depending on her mood, which, she had said, depended on his mood.

"And my father still very much loves my mother, too, and he's still jealous. They been married thirty-some years and he better not see another man looking at her too much. He's one of those men from the old school who saw a woman and decided that he wanted her and nobody else. He told her he wanted her and wouldn't take no for an answer. He's very stubborn, and he decided that it was her he wanted. She was a waitress in this place where he was the cook. He was a good cook and he used to make pretty good money, but when he came from down South he couldn't read or write. He still had to sign his paychecks with an X.

"My father had dropped out of school in the third grade to work in the field so that his younger brothers and sisters could go to school. I don't think he ever blamed my grandparents for that, but you can imagine how he felt, because he was a good cook and a very handsome man, who couldn't read. Can you imagine such a good-looking man who can't read or write his name? That's why I say you've got some very bitter black men out there.

"My mother was the one who taught him to read and write. She's from Connecticut. Even now, my father works very hard and sometimes he blows off steam, comes home cussing and what not. My mother works hard too, but she understands the changes that a black man has to go through. She had two sons die in a period of two years, so she knows.

"One brother was shot by the police, and the other one died of suspicious circumstances also. He died of a supposed overdose, but I know Billy wasn't using heroin, and he only had one needle mark on him, so we think someone OD'd him. To a certain extent this could have made both of us bitter. But I'm glad it didn't, because a bitter woman could have ruined Joe, misused him, because he's basically too trusting. I'm glad I got him before he fell into the wrong hands." She laughed.

"We've been married five years. I don't mean to say we have one of those unreal relationships where there're no problems. We have our problems, but I'm very much in love. Oh, yes.

"I don't like to talk my man up too much, but he's a very beautiful person. He writes poetry, and I used to write poetry, poetry about love and about my children," she said. "He writes poetry about things he sees in the world and how he looks at things. He writes poems about me, and I write poems about him. For example, I've always had beautiful pregnancies, and he wrote me poems about that, about my pregnancies."

"So you're very happy?"

"As a person, yes. As a person I'm very happy." She stretched like a lazy cat. "I was raised to be a wife."

"And that's what you are. You like staying at home?"

"No, that's why I started college. I'm the first one in my family to go to college. My husband was the first one in his family to go, I think. Being a wife and going to school is tough, but I got two more years and I feel I can make it—getting up at six-thirty in the morning and getting four people out is rough. Then I have to get ready. They walk to the train. Every morning I have to run to the train," she said.

I looked at her. She did not seem strong. She seemed very soft for being as thin as she was. It was apparent that she had not defeated suffering. She had let it come into her. The sadness of her life, the deaths of her brothers, the poverty had dropped inside the darkness of her and disappeared.

15
Making Do

Getting it without giving it isn't easy, but we try.

Goldie's is full and busy now. Waitresses and waiters race back and forth to the kitchen to bring out large trays of steaming, colorful food. The candle-lit air is perfumed, but each time the kitchen door swings open, in drifts the delectable odor of cooking pork: soul food. Goldie's is famous for that. The food has changed a lot, however, from years ago, when Goldie's was a greasy spoon.

The décor is exquisite. Evelyn likes it here. I tell her about the garden in back, where, in summer, you can dine alfresco if not exactly under the stars (since stars are not visible in the tiny patch of murky, dark sky that opens above the wall of brick and fire escapes that tower on each side of the tiny garden).

"But it's nice: candlelight and open air," I say.

"Yes," she says. "I like it here. The atmosphere is nice."

About three years ago, Goldie's turned sophisticated, so that chitterlings are now served with parsley, and ham hocks are seasoned with sage. Pig's feet lie on my plate. She despises pork. Shrimp lie on hers. I reach across to take a shrimp to see her reaction, to see if that is too uncouth for her.

She doesn't react. She is a small woman; she is like soul food turned sophisticated. Born and reared in Harlem, she dropped out of high school at sixteen but three years later hooked up a deal to go to college without a diploma. She became a part of one of those Ivy League outreach programs, from which she hustled a full scholarship to Brown University.

She went there for a year before busting out, flunking not because she didn't have the brains to do freshman chemistry, which she got an F in, but because she couldn't make the adjustment from big city to small town, from tenement to ivy dormitory.

She returned to New York but did not go back to Harlem. She settled instead on the edge, on Riverside Drive, from where she forays downtown to Lincoln Center to see Nureyev and Fonteyn dance *The Nutcracker*, or to the Met to hear Leontyne Price sing. On the eight thousand dollars per year she earns as a data-control clerk, she manages to buy a surprising amount of her clothes at Saks Fifth Avenue. Elegant little lady.

She chews in small bites and dabs her mouth with the linen napkin. She smiles. She is enjoying her food. She chews it well. She seems to have made a good mix of her limited budget and expensive taste. She seems now to be a contradictory dish, like some of those that Goldie's serves, like catfish vinaigrette.

"I'll get Frank to bring me here," she says. "Or maybe I'll bring him here for his birthday if he knows how to behave." Her accent suggests North Carolina, where her mother is from.

"Suppose he has to spend his birthday with his wife and kids," I ask.

"Then, we can make it the day before or the day after. No matter." She waves her hand elegantly, as if the fact that he has a wife and child is no more than a mere bothersome fly.

"Frank said you can only love married men."

"I didn't go to fall in love with a married man; Frank knows that. But since I did, it's not the worst thing that ever happened to me. Single men are full of shit."

"How can you say that?"

"They are." Someone at another candle-lit table laughs at whatever his lady friend has said. His giant face looks demonic in the flickering light. His laughter distracts us for a moment. "Most single men are too much in love with themselves to love anybody, shit."

"Well, a single man these days has so many women to date that he can be selective," I say.

"And if he gets my age, in his thirties, and he's not married and he knows you haven't been either, he acts like he's doing you a favor when he gives you some of his time." She never talks with the least bit of food in her mouth. Little gulps of water are necessary between bites of food and bits of conversation. I wonder if she is always like this or has the occasion made her more formal.

"So that's what Frank was saying: you got a jones for married men."

"There ain't no single ones out here to date when you count

the black men on dope and in prison and in Vietnam, and then there's the ones who are sleeping with each other," she laughs.

Almost on cue, a youngish black man strolls in with an older white woman. "And those," she says, alluding to the young man walking goofily along behind the maître d'. "Traitor," Evelyn hisses between her teeth, almost loud enough for the man to hear.

"Any good black man who is in his thirties and single is spoiled. And if you're in your thirties he thinks you're looking for a husband, even if you're not. So he's gon act shitty. So I just decided to share some other woman's man with her. She probably don't care anyway. Both of the married men I love have wives who don't really care about them."

"Both?"

"Oh, I forgot to tell you. I'm in love with two men, two married men," she laughs. "Jimmy and Frank."

"Damn!" I say.

"What can I say?" she asks, laughs, and shrugs her shoulders as if the other man's wife is no more than another bothersome fly. "Single men are full of shit." She looked over at the big-faced man at the next table. "Look at him; can't you just see how much he loves himself! Don't he act like it!"

"How do you know he's single?" I ask.

"He's single, or at least that ain't his wife. They're having too much fun."

The big-faced man laughs again. He is more expensively dressed than his lady friend. He *does* look as though he loves himself. Every so often, the gold pendant at his neck catches the candlelight and sends off a glint of bright yellow light.

"Okay," I say. "He's single, or that's *not* his wife."

"I think a lot of single ladies go with married men." Her fork is ever so delicately poised in her hand. She has regained her composure. Her small mouth chews delicately on the last of her Shrimp Scampi. The candlelight picks up the red in her light complexion. Her mother is from the region of North Carolina where whites, blacks, and Indians mixed freely. Indian blood shows in her color and her cheekbones.

Making Do   203

"I was going with a married man when I met Frank. I had been going with Jimmy for four years. I've always been very much in love with him. Then Frank came along and he wouldn't leave me alone. He kept after me, and I began to like some of his qualities and I started going out with him because Jimmy couldn't be with me as much as I needed. Then I started falling in love with Frank. When this happened I begged Frank to let me alone, but he wouldn't. So I fell deeply in love with him, but I couldn't give Jimmy up.

"I learned from this that it's possible to love, really love, two people at the same time. I didn't know you could do that, but you can. You love each of them for different reasons. Frank and Jimmy. They should make a song out of that," she giggled. "That's the nice thing about being single; you can have two lovers. That's the nice thing about loving married men. In my case both Jimmy and Frank know about each other but they can't complain. How could they? They both have wives at home."

"I think it all goes back to what her father did to her," Frank had said when I talked to him. He walked as he talked. He strutted around his giant living room, obviously proud of the things he had bought for his family. Blue carpet ran out the living room door and surrounded an island of blue marble tile in the hallway, then ran into the dining room under a large Louis XV dining room table with eight chairs.

Against the dining room wall, visible only partially from where I sat in the living room, was a Louis XV sideboard. These period pieces were matched by the giant TV-stereo combination in the same style.

"Her father went off and left her—them (she has three brothers and a sister) when she was a little girl. I guess she used to think about him a lot, because as a child she never saw him the whole time she was growing up. This has had an effect on her."

Frank's home is in Teaneck, New Jersey. He sings baritone for the New Jersey Choral Society, but this is not the way he makes his living. He does this on a strictly voluntary basis, one night a week, two nights a week when the society is preparing for a specific concert.

Frank works in New York City at a sales-promotion firm. "See, Evelyn, though she won't admit it, is too mistrustful of men to let any man get close to her."

As I looked around his house I wondered why he had consented to an interview in which he would admit that he had an outside girl friend. I wondered why he wasn't afraid that his wife would take him to court, charge him with adultery, and dispossess him of everything he owns.

Perhaps Evelyn was right: his wife didn't care. He said, "Speak freely. My wife's at work; the kids are in school."

"You sure it's all right? I don't want to be hauled in as a witness in a divorce proceeding."

He simply laughed. "I think it's a kind of unconscious reaction Evelyn gets. If I try to get close to her she starts moving toward this other married dude she dates, Jimmy McCallister. I know him. I met him once, by accident, but I know him. She got a picture of him on her dresser. He's her main man. He *must* be, because she doesn't have a picture of me up there. His toothbrush is on the rack in the bathroom. Mine is hidden behind the cotton swabs in the medicine cabinet. That's okay, though. I'm glad it's hidden. The dude might do something nasty to my toothbrush," he said, and laughed. His jovial yellowish face holds laughter for a long time.

"But if he starts getting close to her I can feel her moving toward me. She says that's because she doesn't want to give either of us up. I think it's because she doesn't want to give herself up. She's afraid of marriage, but not of love. She loves love. In some ways she's a one-man woman, a wifey type. Believe me, she basically is not a party girl. She almost never goes out alone. She basically likes to relate to one man. She just happened to get caught by two.

"She'd make a nice wife if she wasn't afraid and mistrustful. One thing is, she's basically a very generous person. All her life she's gonna be caught by one man after another. She's not strong enough to pull away and set her own course, so there's a gold mine of love that some guy is forever going to be getting on the q.t."

"Traitor," she hisses at another black man, who comes into Goldie's with a blonde on his arm. We sit waiting for the waiter to take away our empty plates.

"This is Greenwich Village," I say. "What do you expect?"

She laughs. "Frank is nice," she says. "He's full of shit, but he's a nice person. He lies all the time. Be careful when you talk to him. He makes up little stories to entertain himself, but he never consciously tries to mislead you or make you think that he's planning to get a divorce and leave home. So even though he lies about some things he's actually a very honest person. He lies about the number of girl friends he has, but this is just a way of putting you on guard that he's not the most faithful person in the world."

"I talked to him out at his house last week," I say.

"I know; he told me," she says. "What did he say, the dog?"

"He said he's in love. That's one thing he said."

"Of course," she says confidently.

"With his wife," I say, joking.

She laughs. "I know it. I know it. I'm surprised he admitted it, but I've told him that before."

"I was only joking, just to see your reaction."

"He loves his wife. She might not love him, but he loves her."

"We talked about his definition of love. He's really sentimental," I say.

"He is?" she asks, then decides not to make a joke of it. "Yes, he is. He's very sensitive. Most men are not nearly so sensitive. He's insecure—that's why he runs around; and too, he's very hot-natured. Jimmy is different. He's more settled, more sure of himself. He doesn't say much, but I think silence is a form of dishonesty. Jimmy has never lied to me, as far as I know. Frank lies all the time, but I seem to trust Frank more.

"I'm attracted to Jimmy for different reasons. I can't explain all the reasons, but I tell you one thing: he's the only man who ever turned me on by the way he looks. When I first saw him I was attracted to him sexually even before I talked to him. And this had never happened to me before. I usually have to get to know you before I get any sexual feelings one way or another about you. But when I first saw Jimmy at my girl friend's house, I got turned on. It's not his looks, exactly. He's not handsome. Most people would say that Frank is a better-looking man, but there is something very rugged and sexy about him.

"In fact, I get more turned on now by looking at him than by making love to him." Goldie's is famous for desserts. The waiter wheels a cart full of pecan, sweet-potato, apple, pump-kin, mince-meat, lemon and chocolate chiffon pies and pineap-ple upside-down cakes, fresh strawberries, peach cobbler, and puddings. The cart is as high as the waiter, and Evelyn has to stand up to see everything that is there. She wants to keep her weight down. She selects some fresh strawberries without sugar or cream.

I want to keep my weight down too, but I can't resist a piece of deep-dish apple pie à la mode.

"Jimmy makes love like he looks, very rough, not rough, ex-actly, but he needs a lot of physical satisfaction, when some-times all a woman wants is to be held, to be cuddled. You know, that's the hardest part about being in love with two men, getting used to the way each one makes love. And the worst part is being with one and thinking about the other. That's starting to happen to me. The two men are so different. Jimmy likes to make love all night, eight nights a week if pos-sible. That's a big friction point between us. And I like a man who verbalizes his feelings.

"If you try to talk to Jimmy about anything, he won't tell you anything. He'd rather buy you a gift than tell you he loves you. He just doesn't say much. He'd think I was crazy, giving out his name like this. Frank doesn't care. He's not secretive about anything. He doesn't care. He has a weird marriage. I think his wife listens in on the extension phone when he's talking to me."

Making Do   207

"Bullshit," Frank said. "Evelyn talks a lot of shit she don't know. Don't believe that broad. I know what she says. She doesn't understand how I get as much freedom as I do. I get it because I earn it. I worked hard for it. I go into my office whenever I have work to do. I leave when I'm finished. I don't punch a clock. If I want to go out of town, I catch a plane and go. If I want to stay out late at night, I stay. I've got a pretty sweet thing set up for myself.

"People don't understand that. I'm in the streets two or three night a week. I like variety. What can I say? I'm a very hot-natured person. If a woman looks at me in a certain way I get a hard on. I love women. I've always been that way. But love per se, I don't know about love per se. I just like to enjoy life, that's all. Now more than ever, since I turned thirty. Before, I didn't have the means, financial or otherwise, to satisfy my desire to put my dick in various women. Now I've got the means. I use it." He has a golf putter behind his Louis XV-style piano. He pulled it out and started putting golf balls across his thick carpet toward the opening in a shiny brass wood scuttle on the hearth of his fireplace.

"I love my wife. Sincerely. You might not believe that, but I love her very much. You'd have to know more about me to know how I can make that statement in view of what you already know about me." He laughed. None of the four putted golf balls reached the hearth.

"You'd have to know about how I was raised and how the first years of our marriage went before you could understand that.

"I didn't do well with women when I was younger. I always had this need for love that I never got, when I was younger. I didn't start to look like a man until I was past thirty. Up to then I looked like a cute little boy. Women would like me but they didn't love me and therefore would never give what I really wanted," he said.

He did look young to be thirty-four. His eyes were young. He dressed young—black-and-white tee shirt with Aztec design embroidered in red and yellow about an inch below the neck line. The embroidery work was partially covered by love beads.

He didn't look like the owner of a five-bedroom home, or the father of three school-aged daughters. He did, however, look like a man who would not have sons, only daughters. Cute daughters, who could, at will, crawl all over their father, kiss him, push him, mess up his hair, treat him as a pal as well as a parent.

"Cute. That nigger was never cute. You saw him," she says and laughs. This restaurant is not as elegant as Goldie's. It is a new "in" spot among Indian restaurants in New York. People like it because of the informal atmosphere. Men don't have to wear jackets and ties even for dinner. "He looks all right but I wouldn't classify him as cute," she says. "He thinks he's cute. It's true he looks like a little boy—big head, long neck, skinny. The only difference now is he looks like a fat little boy. I guess you could say he's pudgy and cute. He's just as cute as Jimmy. Jimmy isn't cute. They both look okay. I don't choose a man because he looks good. I fall in love for other reasons. I fall in love for very idealistic reasons, even though everyone is always telling me that I'll never find the perfect love. I guess that's what I'm looking for, a perfect love.

"I have this very fantastic picture of how I want love to be: candle-lit dinner for two, white linen tablecloth, me in a long white gown, he in a tuxedo, Johnny Mathis on stage. It takes place at the Plaza. We would go to bed after the show but we wouldn't make love. He would just hold me in his arms. Jimmy and Frank think I'm crazy because I just want to be held sometimes. I don't want to make love, I just want to be held.

"That could be one reason why I might not get married. I want it to be perfect when I get married, and everyone knows that nothing is ever perfect. I would hate to have children and then have the marriage break up. But I know me. If it wasn't working out I would have to leave. I wouldn't stay together

Making Do 209

just for the kids' sake. I grew up without a father and it didn't hurt me.

"But I don't think I'll find the perfect man, anyway. When I see a fault in Jimmy I start thinking about Frank, because he might not have this particular fault, but then when I see a fault in Frank and I'm with him I start thinking about Jimmy. I had to stop myself from doing that, because it got so bad that every time I was with one of them I was wishing I was with the other.

"Right now if both of them asked me to marry, I would choose one but the minute I did I would begin thinking that I had chosen the wrong one. I don't ever want to make any choice that will last forever.

"If they forced me to choose I would probably choose Jimmy. I would choose him on the basis that I think he loves *me* more. Frank tells me more often that he loves me, but I think Jimmy loves me with a deeper love. He shows me that he loves me, and I can feel that he loves me but he won't say it. He's so detached sometimes. I know he can't be lying there with nothing on his mind. I asks what he thinks. I want to know what it is. Even if I get only a hint of what he's thinking about, I want that. I want to tell him everything on my mind, but I have to hold back because he doesn't say what's on his.

"He gets embarrassed very easily, and if I say, 'I love you,' it embarrasses him. He doesn't know how to accept it. I think he mistrusts words when his feelings are involved. He believes in noises: moaning and groaning," she laughs. "That's the only way I know I'm doing something that he likes. He moans louder or groans louder. He never says.

"Words have to have some meaning. But when he's in a love-making situation he says they're meaningless. There's always music. He's never relaxed without some music playing, unless there's a ball game on, and sometimes the lyrics of a song will say something and he'll say; 'Check out that song. That's me and you' or 'That's the way I feel about you.' In fact he can say sweeter things to me on the telephone than he can in person.

"I mistrust words too, but you can use the same words that

are common and if they correspond to the feeling that's going through your body, then they mean something. You get a positive interpretation of them and you can be sure they're true. I'm not trying to say I want a running conversation. That would throw me off, too. I just want to know what goes on in his mind.

"I love him but I have to accept the shell that he places around himself. That's what I mean when I say that he can't love completely. He can't give himself completely over a long period of time. But not just him; I've noticed it in other men. They have a lot of love to give but they're afraid to let it come out. They give you bits and pieces, and then it seems like a game. You want to give your love totally, but you end up playing this game too, because he's playing it.

"It might have something to do with his background. His mother wasn't very affectionate. She couldn't afford to be. She had to raise three boys by herself. This made her cold. She gave up everything for those boys. I think she gave up too much. She didn't date. She didn't have a social life. She's cold, and he's cold except when he's making love.

"Now, his mother is very affectionate toward *his* children, her grandchildren. She doesn't have the responsibility of raising them, so she can be affectionate. I must say that she did a good job of raising Jimmy and his two brothers. None of them are in prison or on dope. But I wish she had treated them like she does her grandchildren. They would have felt freer to give love. Then Jimmy would be perfect, because when he makes love you feel how intense and hungry he is. It reassures you that he really wants you.

"I wish you could interview him. I'd like to know what goes on in his mind. I'd like to know what he feels. I know all about Frank. In a way, Frank had a rougher time than either Jimmy or I. He didn't have a mother *or* father," she said.

This time, I met Frank in Brooklyn after he had returned from playing golf out on Long Island. The day was a bit cold but he was a golf nut. He had gone with a client to a country club out by Hempstead, and the client had dropped him off at his mother-in-law's house in Brooklyn. I told him that while we talked I could drive him back to Manhattan, where he had left his car.

"Evelyn said you didn't have a father, or mother either."

"Yeah, I lived with my stepfather. My mother died when I was young, and at the time, she was living with this man who wasn't actually married to her but I call him my stepfather. He raised me and I guess he did the best he could. We were very poor when we were young. It was him, me, and my older brother," he said. We stopped at a traffic light and watched the cars racing across in front of us on the cross street.

"I remember, the apartment we had didn't even have a door on it. There was a quilt hanging across the doorway and all you had to do was push back the quilt to get inside. Someone had to stay home all the time to keep neighbors from coming in and stealing anything of value. I stayed there until I was sixteen, and then I joined the Army. I got to travel a little and see the world, but I came right back to Harlem. That was the only home I knew." The traffic light changed. We started down the long stretch toward the Brooklyn Bridge.

"I was nineteen, almost twenty, when I got out. The only thing to do was bum around the streets. It took me a long time to get my head straight. I met this woman. She was on welfare, had two children, practically illiterate she was; she could barely read the labels on canned food. Lucky they had pictures on most food. She would open peas when she wanted carrots, without the labels. I fell deeply in love with her and moved into her place." The iron grates of the bridge made the tires sing.

"We lived together until the father of one of her babies took her to court to try to get custody of his child. He called her an unfit mother because she had me, a teen-aged boy, living with her and she was somewhere in her thirties.

"So she had to put me out to save her child custody. I was very hurt by that, because I loved her very much and wanted to help her. Before I recovered, I met my wife. She was very religious. I got a job. I didn't mind going to church three times a week. I minded, but I did it to keep her happy." The picture of his wife that he carried in his wallet showed a stern-faced, oriental-looking woman.

"We saved our money and bought a little house. Then, just when we got into the house, I lost my job and at the same time she got pregnant. I used to sit around the house all day and she would bitch about me not working, but I think during that time she loved me more than she ever did. I kept losing jobs. I had a job as a messenger for Macy's and I lost that. I was the only person ever to lose a job at the Post Office for incompetency," he laughed. We crossed busy Canal Street and headed up Sixth Avenue.

"My wife had to work two jobs while she was seven months pregnant, but that wasn't the thing that broke us up; I think she liked that. Strange enough, she was happy bitching at me every day. She would bring the money home to support us— pay the rent, buy the food. I think what it was is that as long as I wasn't working she could control my habits by controlling all the money.

"Our marriage didn't start to go bad until I started to get on my feet. Rather than lay around the house, I decided to go to Queens Community College. She started saying that she wasn't going to work two jobs to pay for me to go to school, but that was phony, because school was free. In fact, I was getting some money from the GI Bill, and anyway, it was better than laying around.

"She had the baby and she wanted me to stay home and watch it, but after a while I got a job and was working and going to school full time, which was okay because her mother didn't mind keeping the baby for free. Her mother liked me. So my wife couldn't use the baby-sitting as an excuse, so she began to challenge me in other ways. She started to imply that I was a faggot because I was always reading books. At that time I had fallen in love with romantic poetry and I was always reading it, and she would say that I was a faggot for running around reading poetry.

"Now, this was only a two-year school, but the closer I got to graduation the more pressure she put on me: 'Why don't you just leave?' That's what she'd say. 'Just leave, Frank.' Or when I came home she'd say something like: 'Oh, you came back. What for?'

"She cut me off sexually and then started accusing me of being a homosexual for not making love to her. She wouldn't let me make love to her and then she'd blame me for not making love to her. There was entirely too much confusion for me, so I started hanging out.

"I still loved her. That's why I say that I still love her. I don't think she really knew what she was doing. It was all subconscious. Then I met this Romanian Jewish woman at Queens College. I started going up to her apartment. It was a place where I could relax, a place where I didn't have to *be* anything. She was the kind of woman that all I had to be is black and that would satisfy her. So I moved in with this woman.

"She was much older than me too, just like the woman on welfare. I stayed with her about nine months. She lived in a big old dusty apartment on West End Avenue, full of antiques and stuff. It was really a weird scene. When I made love to her she would start speaking in Romanian. It was funny.

"I got tired of that, so I moved in with this black lady in the Bronx. Meanwhile, just as soon as I moved out on my wife she had the house completely redone for eight thousand dollars, just to show me that she could do okay by herself. She got a new bathroom, new kitchen cabinets, new kitchen appliances, wall-to-wall carpeting—the whole thing. Now, all this time I was going back home every once in a while to see my daughters. My wife and I stayed apart for about four years. I transferred to Brooklyn College and finished and got a good job.

"Then my daughters started having trouble in school, and my wife is not too well educated so she couldn't help my daughter with her homework, so I had to go out there three or four times a week to help her with new math and stuff.

"Whenever I stayed late I would stay the night on the sofa and get up early the next morning and come to work. Gradually me and my wife started sleeping together. I guess I was the one who wanted it, because I was still in love with her.

And gradually I started moving back in. I like being around my daughters; we have a nice thing going. I feel very close to them. I have never felt very close to my wife. She ignores me as much as she can, but she's courteous. She gives me the respect that a man is due. All her friends think we get along well.

"And of course she appreciates the fact that I'm making good money and can keep up the bills so she can use her money to shop at Bloomingdales and Saks Fifth Avenue. She has her little dishwasher and the clothes washer and dryer right there in the house. These are the things that are important to her.

"Just before I came back home, I had met Evelyn. For a long time we used to just talk, and sometimes I would call her from home. All my wife wanted to do in the evening was look at television and get her hair set so she would look nice when she went out to work the next day. She had worked her way up to supervisor; her job was the only thing that really mattered to her. We moved up to a bigger and better house; that's the house we own now: seventy thousand dollars.

"This all could make you feel like less than a man if you didn't have another woman who paid attention to you and acted like she needed you, and bought things for you instead of for herself, presents and little things."

"Like I said, Frank has had a very strange life, but haven't we all?" The skinny Indian waiter brings the check. "I've been on my own nearly all of my life," Evelyn says. "I don't like it but I'd rather be by myself than listen to a lot of jive or a lot of lies. If it's one thing I can't stand it's to be lied to, and men are terrible liars. Even when there's no call to lie, they lie. Before I met Jimmy I had a boy friend who was single. His name was Tyrone Powell. He was trying to play two or three women at once, so he had to lie a lot to try and keep them all on the string.

"When someone lies to you, that's the worst insult in the world. That's just like saying, 'This chick is stupid; I can tell her anything.' That's what this fellow did. He would not show up for a date and then, when he'd finally call, he'd tell you a story that even a baby couldn't believe. He was that way from when I first met him, but I liked him because he was fun to be with. We used to party a lot in Harlem or up in the Bronx.

"With him it was like being a teen-ager all over again. He knew a lot of the people I had grown up with, so we had a good time at parties and such. I don't know how he did it, but he got me to liking him enough to let him move in with me. We lived together for about nine months.

"But living together was boring. We actually had more fun when we were living apart. We went out more. We did more things. We had more to talk about. When we started living together, we used to walk around the apartment all evening without saying a word to each other.

"I don't think we ever should have lived together, but it was a thing where we each were very jealous. He didn't want me seeing this fellow named Outlaw, who was interested in me, and there was a little, skinny blonde chasing him, and I hated to think of him being with a whitey.

"So we started living together just as a way of limiting each other's freedom. It wasn't a thing of us really wanting to live together. I just didn't want him going out with that girl. I guess that shows that inwardly I'm very jealous even though I don't show it. I'm jealous because inwardly I'm very insecure, too.

"It's been a thing of, if a man is with me and he has to run around it makes me feel that I'm not enough woman for him. It makes me feel inadequate. Maybe that's one reason why I don't mind married men. When they're not with me I can at least tell myself that they're with their wives—not because they love their wives more than me but because of a legal obligation or because of the kids."

We get our coats and walk out into the cool Manhattan night. "And another thing I think is that love and sex have to go together, and Tyrone was the kind of man who would have sex with a snake if someone would hold the snake's head. He was very free sexually, and I am only as long as I feel that a man belongs to me. If I think he's mine and mine alone I'll do anything for him or with him, but the minute I begin to feel unsure of him I freeze up. I can't help it.

"I'm like that. If I don't have someone of my own it's almost like I am frigid. I have gone for more than a year without having sex with anyone. People run around acting like sex was the greatest thing ever invented. It isn't unless you're with someone you love. I believe that. I believe in love, but I don't think love has ever been as beautiful as I've dreamed it would be.

"I was in Nassau for a week with Jimmy once and that was the closest I've ever come to a perfect love. Jimmy and I still talk about it.

"I had him all to myself. It was like I owned him. He didn't know anyone there and there was nowhere either of us could go. I felt so secure. I made love to him as I have never made love before or since. He couldn't believe it. I just wanted more and more of him. I just wanted to eat him up, to consume him. This was shortly after I met Jimmy, shortly after Tyrone and I broke up. What happened with Tyrone and I was this:

"We were living together and losing all our feelings for each other. I knew he was playing around and this made me almost frigid. Then, one time, I saw him up on 145th Street getting out of a car with this girl. I had seen the girl before, so I figured that this must be one of his women. I asked him about it when he came home, but he kept denying that I saw him. Like I'm supposed to be too big a fool to know what I saw.

"I wouldn't have been so mad if he'd admitted he was with the girl. I was as close to both of them as I am to that pole. It was broad daylight. I know it was him, but he had made up in his mind he was going to deny it no matter what. I got so mad I couldn't see straight. I put my fist through the mirror on the bathroom door but I was so mad that it didn't hurt. I told him to get out. I was screaming and my hand was bleeding. I must have been hysterical, because he got out and he didn't even come back to get his clothing. He sent his friend back to pick up his clothes.

"A long time after that, we went out a couple of times to-gether but I could never feel close to him again. I froze up on him. We were friends, but I could never make love to him.

"Then I met Jimmy, and he and I had a good thing, until Frank came along and wouldn't give up. He kept after me and after me until I finally gave in to him. He had more free time than Jimmy, so he and I used to hang out together in the sum-mertime. In Central Park and down in the Village. He lied a lot but I don't think he did it to deceive. I think he does it to hide his true feelings. I think if he really told himself the truth, he would go crazy."

16
Who Can Say?

If it's what I like, who can say it's wrong?

"I've had some beautiful men in my day," Clara said. "I've always had a weakness for beautiful things. I love beautiful men. That's what love means to me: something good to look up at. I'm sorry, but I can't love nothing ugly. I won't even ride in a ugly car, much less let a ugly man get in bed with me. I can't do it. Who wants to be looking up at something ugly?" The smoke from her cigarette curled up toward her eyes. She pulled back from it and coughed as she laughed. The place was quiet, especially in the booth back near the counter, where we were sitting.

"That's the way I am. People love for different reasons. Right? That's my reason. A man could be rotten as hell; just as long as he looks good, I can fall in love with him; and he could be nice as hell and if he's not good-looking I could never love him. You might say that's wrong, but that's the way I am.

"This man I got now. This man I love right now, he's got looks that would put Harry Belafonte to shame. Billy Dee Williams would be glad to trade looks with him, if he could. Who? He's fine, honey. I'm not lying. You think I'm lying. I wish I had a picture to show you. I love him to death. I love being around him. I love for him to touch me. I love to do for him." Her voice rose with the ecstasy of thinking about him. She tried to laugh, but cigarette smoke choked her.

"Where'd you meet him?" I asked and sipped on the iced tea she had handed me from the waitress station just behind her.

"I met him in here," she said. "When this place is busy I see a lot of men coming in here. They come downstairs sometimes to have a drink. Maybe they're in bad shape. Maybe their old lady didn't fix supper for them. So they come up here to have a bite to eat. You can bet if a man comes up here to eat alone there's something wrong. So if he's worth talking to, I might strike up a conversation," she said, still puffing on her cigarette. Her back was against the wall instead of against the back of the booth. One leg was stretched out along the seat. The cushion on the seat was covered with a red-and-white oil cloth.

Who Can Say?

"Late at night, there may not be much of anybody up here but him and me, and so I strike up a conversation. I give him a kind of display of what I got." She had on a tight little waitress' white uniform, the skirt of which rode high on her big, dark thighs. The thigh that was stretched out along the seat was smooth and shapely under her sheer, sexy hose.

Her buttocks were ample, I remembered, and she had the tiniest waist; and then there was the way the slick polyester of her uniform slid with every movement she made, whistled against the taffeta of her slip when she reached or walked or stretched. She was thirty-seven, but her body could pass for eighteen. She was an easy woman to interview, because she was a sassy, non-stop talker. The scene was nice. It was late at night. You have to picture it to appreciate it.

The restaurant, the Blue Angel, is deserted now except for an arguing couple up front near the heavily draped picture window. The neon window sign is barely visible through the drapes. "I don't know how I got that way. My mother said I was like that as a baby," she says. "When black dolls first came out, my mother said I wouldn't play with one. Every man I've ever been involved with is light-skinned.

"I've paid the price for my habit. I've loved men who I was sure didn't love me, who were just using me. I didn't care, I just like to look at a nice-looking man. I've always been funny that way." She is not light-skinned herself, but she is not as ugly as she feels. Her feelings of ugliness are based on her low opinion of her Africanesque features—not the Nubian features of smooth skin and high cheekbone, not the haunting beauty of the African mask, not even the soft, feminine darkness of the girl who is arguing with her man at the front table.

She has rude features, true: the lips, the nose doesn't fit well beneath the shoulder-length, shiny wig. She is thick-tongued when she speaks. "I have a mirror. I can look in the mirror. I can see. I know men. I know what they want. You can't tell me. I've been out here for fifteen years. I came to New York when I was twenty years old and I been dealing out here daily for seventeen years. I know what I like and I do whatever I gotta do to get it. If I could have children I would love to have a child by this man I got now.

"The reason I get so many good-looking men is that I know how to treat a man. If I got to, I'll go out and work for a man. If I have to work two jobs, I do that. I'll kiss a man's ass to keep him if he's what I want. I'm not ashamed to do that. I don't care. What does it mean? That's what love is to me, to me, being with someone you love being with."

"Why you put yourself down, though?"

"I don't put myself down. You asked me a direct question and I answered it. I don't put myself down, because I *know* I can get more men than—" She stops and looks at the couple arguing. She whispers, "I never argue with a man. A man's gonna do what he wants to anyway and he'll come to see you if he wants to, if you got something that he wants. Even though I might kiss a man's ass if he comes, I would never ask him to come in the first place. That's his decision, and I'd never ask him to stay if he didn't want to stay.

"I'll tell you how it used to be with me: It would be a thing where a man would move in with me and stay. Maybe he was having some kind of problem. Maybe he was just breaking up with his wife. He falls in love. He falls in love because I do everything that a man needs.

"I don't mean I let him walk on me. It's not like that. I don't want to give the wrong idea. I just be very good to him. If I like what a man looks like, I just naturally be good to him. I can get into a man's mood. Whatever his problem is, I can help him bring it out, put it out on the table and deal with it. Then, after he gets himself together, he leaves. It hurts. It hurts, but you can't let a person stay sick just so you can keep that person. That would mean you're sicker than he is.

"But I don't look at it as a man using me and leaving me with nothing. Whatever I learn from one man I use it to help someone else," she says. I look at her. Her voice is kind. She is not that bad-looking. I wonder if her looks are the real reason that men leave her. I wonder if she really wants to keep any of them. I wonder if it's something about her not being able to have children, but she says that that has nothing to do with it. I wonder if she really knows the reason.

She gets up to serve dessert and coffee to the arguing couple up front. "Maybe you don't really want a permanent man," I say again when she sits back down. She has lit another cigarette. Most of her cigarettes are never taken down from her mouth until they are smoked up. They remain between her lips, sending smoke up toward her sad, yellowing eyes.

"No, that's not right," she says; "in fact this man that I have right now. There's a good chance that he and I will stay together.

"For how long? Until when?"

"For a long time. He works down from here. He works the late shift selling subway tokens at the 135th Street station. We been together for almost a year. I don't say I love him more than I loved any other man, but I know him better. I know his habits and I think he might stay.

"For how long?

"How do I know? But I can tell he loves me. There's a certain kind of hurt you get being under, enjoying a man who don't love you. A certain kind of good feeling just looking at him, wishing you could have him, rubbing his face, loving him. But with a man who loves you, you might not get that same feeling. You get a more peaceful feeling. That's what I get from the man I'm with now. That's the reason I love him. We been together for over a year. He's not that good in bed. So it's not a sexual thing that attracts you. It's just a matter of loving to be with him. I would never cheat on him. The idea that he owns me makes him feel secure with me.

"I know men, and it all depends on what you can make a man feel toward hisself. For example, I think his wife is frigid. He never told me this in so many words, but I picked it up from things he says. I listen to everything a man says, because a man will never tell you what he really wants you to know, but then, when it comes time to deal with him, he expects you to know.

"So when he deals with me I know he wants me to make him think he's a good man, that he's a good lover. He wants to feel that about hisself. He is a good lover, in a way. Every man is, in his way, if you love being with him and you can respond and accept the way he is.

"I make love with my eyes open, because I like to see what I'm getting. That can inspire me to make a man feel good about himself, because if he's good-looking, I can get off just looking at him. I guess that's why I can't make love to no ugly man. I can't lie to him and tell him how pretty he is, and I like to do that when I'm loving a man.

"You know, I been in love with a lot of men in my lifetime, but I never been in love with more than one at a time. I usually concentrate on one man, and this one I've been concentrating on for more than a year.

"If he stays with his wife I'll have him. If he gets a divorce, then he'll probably find a better-looking woman than me. As it is, he don't have to take me anywhere. He can use the excuse that he's married and that he's well known and someone might see us. But I know the reason is he don't necessarily want to be seen with me.

"I know I don't need anybody to tell me that I ain't Lena Horne. I got mirrors. I'm thirty-seven years old and I know what's happening.

"You take a man who's having trouble at home and he finds a woman who'll do anything he wants her to do: fix him good food, wash his armpits—shit.

"One reason this man will always need somebody like me is that he's very selfish. Because of his looks he's gotten everything he wanted. You have to do everything for him. He's always talking about hisself: his problems, his moods, his this and his that. The average woman out here will get tired of him always talking about hisself.

"He makes good money, but he spends it all on hisself. He don't ever buy me nothing to speak of. The only thing he give you for a birthday is a excuse. If he brings you a bunch of flowers he acts like he's brought you a diamond ring. He's something else. His wife spends all his money and she don't give him shit. He don't sleep with her. He sleeps with me. I keep it nice for him at my place.

Who Can Say?   225

"I'm from North Carolina, so I know how to treat a man. I know how to cook and do, and take care of business." She gets up again, so the arguing couple can pay their check and leave. She comes back, tucking her tip in her tight pocket, cigarette still dangling from her lips. "I keep good scotch in there for him, any kind of food he wants, ready-cooked, night clothes in the closet, cologne in the bathroom.

"I work my ass off to pay the rent. He don't put a dime in and I don't ask. I buy the records for the stereo and I make the notes on the stereo and the TV. I work hard for every cent I get, and when I have to work two jobs, I do. Sometimes I tend bar downstairs to make extra money, and I spend every cent on what I enjoy: pretty men. I love pretty men. If you saw my apartment you'd see. I ought to take you up there one time. Everything in it is pretty white: rug. I wouldn't let you walk in shoes on this rug I got. You should see it.

"He has all the luxury at his disposal; that's why he gon be there when I get home. He got the key. His wife and him are going through this thing, so he goes by my place when he gets off. He gets off at twelve.

"He's a pretty Cuban man, who's got this weakness for dark-skinned women. His wife is dark. I think she's frigid or else she's using that to make him insecure. Women do that. She's a slick bitch. I know somebody who knows her. The guy who cooks here knows her because he lives in their building in the Bronx.

"I don't hate her, though. I don't think I'd wanna be married to no man that good-looking, either," she says, alluding again to the fact that she thinks she is ugly. The more she says it the less it seems to fit. Without the wig, with her hair pushed backward she would be rudely attractive. And she must know she has a beautiful body; otherwise, why would she walk as she does? Why would she wear her skirts so short? Why would she wear only polyester that whistles against the shiny taffeta of her slips as she struts her stuff?

17

Another Love Affair

A black woman can never really love a black man,
or vice-versa. . . .

"When he comes in here, you'll see. If he comes in tonight, the minute he comes through the door you'll notice me changing," Cecil says and pulls back the short green drape that covers a high window onto the dance floor. Couples are dancing to the records he has just put on Turntable Three.

"He's fine. You'll know him the instant you see him. He comes here all the time, the beast. He doesn't look like a beast. In fact, he's been a professional model, but he is my beast. I save this one record to play when he comes in. I love to see him dance to it. He knows that I play it for him. He just gets all off on it.

"You can tell a gay man by the way he dances. Even a very masculine man, and, by the way, most gay men are very masculine, which is a contradiction too, since all men are gay men. He always sits over there by the bar."

I go to the window and look out on the floor. Cecil dances a little as he watches. Then he looks back to make sure the other two turntables are set up, set up so that he can switch to one of them without a break, so the music can go on and the fun never stop until 4 A.M., when the place closes.

"See that fellow there with the Nehru-type thing on?" He points to a dancing man.

"The white man?"

"He's not white, he's Latin."

"Okay, I see him."

"I've had him several times," Cecil laughs, "and the girl with him knows it. At least she has strong suspicions. He might come back here later to find out if anything is happening. If it is, he'll drop her at home and double back in a cab."

"He's a good dancer," I say, "but I would never guess that he was gay, any more than anyone else out there."

"They are all gay. One hundred per cent. I told you that."

"Then, this is a gay disco?"

"No, go on. I don't hang out at places like that. Places like that make me sick. I don't like anything that's exclusively this or exclusively the other. Nothing in life is. God, no. Most of the men here would be appalled to hear you say that. Most of these clods have never had an experience, a love experience, with another man, but that's because most of them adhere to the limitations of society. There are so many limitations placed on who you can love. If you're Protestant you can't love Catholic, or vice-versa. If you're black you can't love white, or vice-versa. If you're a man you can't love another man; or woman, a woman. If you're Jewish you shouldn't love gentile—the whole thing leaves me quite ill."

Cecil looks as if he could be part Latin, but he is not. He's simply, as he puts it, "an American-bred yellow nigger from North Carolina." He seems tall until you stand beside him and discover it is his thinness that makes him appear tall. He is only about five nine.

He is the kind of handsome that a "straight" man would pick out as possibly gay, just possibly. But he says he is not homo or bisexual.

"I hate all the terms that society labels things with. I just refuse to limit myself to loving one way. Why should I? You're limited anyway by the fact that you are born and are going to die. Why have any other limitations?" He laughs, claps his hands, and dances. He is an elegant dancer, and he knows it. He slides around inside the music. He goes to the door of the control booth, opens it, looks out, and closes the door. He has not missed a beat.

A petite college-age girl comes into the booth. She has just come in from outside in the cold. She has brought the smell of the cold in with her. Cecil hugs her as she takes off her red coat. "Hey, darling," he says. "This is my little darling." His voice has the lilt that is often associated with homosexuality. He holds the small girl back from him as an appraising mother would. "Let me look at you. You look simply fabulous, fabulous, girl. Look at you."

He introduces her to me. "Sandy, this is George. George, Sandy, Sandy, George," but he doesn't take his appraising eyes off of her. There is something very warm and honest about the way they look at each other, drink each other in. There is a little panic in the look also. They chat about mutual friends. I look toward the outside of the booth, where the dancers are. A tall black man is sweating hard as he works out to the music.

230   *Love, Black Love*

He has a dance step that contains a wide-legged jump. He spins. Other dancers have come onto the floor. A mirrored ball spins above their heads, sending off light in all directions.

Cecil calls to me. The music is not as loud in the booth as it is on the floor outside. "We don't have to stop the interview because Sandy's here. She knows me."

Sandy has just stopped hugging him. "Yes, Cecil, I know you." She prepares to take up her duties as the apprentice D.J.

"You behave, Sandy. This handsome gentleman and I are talking about something you know absolutely nothing about: Love," Cecil says, still dancing and using his handkerchief as a prop. "Ah-h-h-h-h," he says every time the music gets good to him.

The small girl mixes in the music from the turntable. She is a student at Stanford, home for the Christmas holiday. She loves Cecil. Cecil has made love to her, loved her well, small and brown and pretty as she is. She can run the turntables while Cecil talks or goes off to make love.

"This lover that I have now, he'll come in here with his wife, and I'll play the record for him, and he'll know that it's being played for him and he'll dance in a way that'll let me know that he's missed me. When I think of him, I almost feel that I want to be completely homosexual. If he'd pack his bags and leave his wife, I'd leave mine before he got out his door good.

"He's such a hypocrite. The man who owns this place knows that he's my lover. The bartenders and hatcheck girls—everyone. He comes here and waits for me to get off some nights. His mother knows. My wife knows. His wife knows, but men are so dishonest. He has to keep up this pretense that he's part of the mainstream, that he has a wife and two kids. The whole thing leaves me personally very ill." Cecil dances. "Sometimes I think I should just die and give my body to a research foundation," he laughs.

"You're quite conscious of physical appearance. You talk about it quite often," I say. He dances with the little Stanford girl. She is quite pretty too.

"It makes a difference. You could have ever so much to offer but if you look like a gargoyle, God, who's ever going to take the time to notice?" The Stanford girl is deep in the music. It is as if she does not hear him or anything else, as if she is completely unconscious of everything else until it is time to mix in another record.

"But you could be ever so pretty and have nothing to offer," I say.

"True. That's why I like this lover I have now. He's not just a pretty face, but he's such a beast," Cecil laughs.

"Are you happy?"

"No."

"Is he happy?"

"I don't see how he could be. Living with *that* woman."

"Do you know her?"

"Yes."

"Does she know . . ."

"She knows that I love him very— She knows and she doesn't know. She doesn't want to know. All she knows is that he's out with me. Just so she doesn't have to deal with the facts of it, we are together one or two nights a week. He has spent three weeks with me in Montreal, Canada. She knows, but she would rather have him out with me than out with another woman."

"Why?"

"Because she knows that whatever two men do together it will never threaten her relationship."

"Wouldn't she be afraid that he might love you so much that he'd want to move in with you?"

"That's never the fear. That's never the fear. She knows that he doesn't have the guts to be exclusively gay. She knows that the forces of society will always help to keep him in line."

"But you already said that a good part of his society already knows that he is gay. His mother knows that he's gay."

"His mother knows and she doesn't know. I've made love to him right in his mother's house in Harlem."

"Where was she?"

"In the other room."

"Was it a house or an apartment?"

"An apartment."

"Then, how could she even pretend that she doesn't know?"

"She doesn't care. As long as she doesn't have to acknowledge it. As long as she doesn't have to introduce him as 'My son, the gargoyle, da-da-da-dum.'"

"Then, women are not more honest than men?"

"I didn't say they were. I said I have to have relationships with women because they have a greater sense of reality than men. They are freer to express their emotions than men, and women are more attractive to me physically. Sometimes when I'm walking down Fifth Avenue on a sunny day and I catch myself looking at women, exclusively, I have to warn myself, 'Don't be one-sided, Cecil. Start looking at a few men.' But men don't really turn me on, to look at. In the first place, most men have bodies that do not compare with mine.

"I dig women because they give me a reality that I can't get from men, but I don't like to be involved emotionally with women. I could be, but I just don't choose to be."

"Then, why did you get married?"

"It was never something that I wanted. My wife wanted it. I was living with her for about three years. I prefer *living* with women because women can't make certain demands on you."

"Why?"

"They just can't. They can't say, 'You'd better be home at a certain time,' like a male lover tries to do. I love talking to women and relating to them on an intellectual level." He looked back out on the dance floor. "If you want to know the truth: I married her for money, but like everything else this is true and not true."

"Is she wealthy?"

"No. She's white, and white people can do things for you careerwise. At the time, I wanted to be an actor and she was already into acting. Her husband was an actor and she knew a lot of important people in the theater."

"What was so attractive about you that she would leave her husband for you?"

"Look at me. You can see." He posed and laughed. "No, it

was because I was exciting and different and honest. I'm honest about everything but my age."

"I've been trying to guess your age."

"I know." He blushes.

"What is it?"

"I can pass for any age from eighteen to thirty-five. What age do I look?"

"I have no idea."

"I know."

"How does she feel about you being with other men?"

"She prefers that to me being with other women. And another reason I married her was that white people have a higher level of tolerance for any aberration of society."

"I've heard just the opposite."

"It's not true. My mother is black and she doesn't tolerate anything," he laughs.

"Least of all, you," I laugh.

"She tolerates my brother because he's a hypocrite like her. White people are much more tolerant."

"Are there more white homosexuals than black?"

"More acknowledged ones. Black people are extremely conscious of image, which makes me sick. Black people make me sick. Everyone makes me sick. I should decide to be completely homosexual. If you want to know what I really love. I love black men. I'm not talking about creepy black men, and there are plenty of those, but the true black man in these United States," he says.

He is serious now. He has forgotten about the music. The pretty Stanford girl is running the turntables. We sit in the two director's chairs against the wall.

"I feel really sorry for black men in this society. They have this tremendous role-responsibility, tremendous role-pressure. I want to do whatever I can to relieve this, to fill a gap."

"Or have a gap filled," I joke.

"Touché." He smiles only slightly; he is not going to be diverted from his seriousness. "A black man in these United States can never allow any of his softness to show in his personality. He has to be on his guard. My lover had to be tough

234   *Love, Black Love*

or he would have ended up on dope or dead or castrated. . . ."

"What's your lover's name?"

"I don't think I should tell you that."

"I wouldn't use the real name anyway."

"Ok, let's call him Jimmy for conversation's sake."

"Ok, let's call him Jimmy." I am stalling so that his seriousness will not run its course too quickly. I want to stretch it out to get as much out of it as I can.

"Jimmy has survived in the jungles of Harlem since he was eleven. He's been in the streets since he was eleven. He got his first gunshot wound when he was fourteen. He robbed his first store when he was fifteen. He's had to have this image in order to survive. Show weak and the streets will gobble you up.

"You'll see him when he comes in. He's a very tough-looking man. He's been out there. I was raised in the South. It was a much softer life down there, but Jimmy was born in Harlem Hospital. Is that New York, or is that New York? He's New York City cool, but I worked to get behind that supermasculine façade. I worked to give him a place where he could drop this killer role that he has to live up to. He began to change gradually. What signaled it was one time when we were making love. He began screaming, 'Do something to me. Make me do something. Make me do anything you want me to do!' Here he was, a man who had always made people do what he wanted, even at the point of a gun. He had been a pimp and a stick-up man. You name it and he'd done it. Here he was begging for someone to put him through his paces.

"But I didn't. I didn't do anything to humiliate him or to demoralize him. The funny thing is that while he was going through this he was losing his erection, but I didn't let him panic. Then we just started talking. He talked about his childhood and his emotions and his fears. He was able to give vent to so many things that he would never give vent to in front of anyone else.

"Sometimes he would start to talk and he would just start

crying. Not that he was sad. It was sadness and happiness too. I guess it was just relief, so he would cry. We are really close.

"I'm not saying that a woman could not have done this with him. If he could ever have trusted a woman enough. But I don't think he could have trusted a woman enough. He felt that he couldn't show weak in front of a black woman. She would crush him; inadvertently or not, she would use his weakness against him and despise him for being weak. He could not have shown it in front of a white woman because he had too much general mistrust for white people.

"I don't think that at this point in time a woman could really have dealt with it. I can understand the woman's point of view because in some ways I identify with women. Women are my best friends. I am closer to women than most men because they tell me things that they wouldn't tell a so-called straight man. And being a homosexual I feel some of the pressure that a woman feels. I feel it's almost totally impossible for men and women to love each other realistically."

"Why?"

"They never know each other." He slows up and begins to speak cautiously. "I think— I think men, regardless of the man, tend to regard women as inferiors, and I don't care who the man is. I don't care how many women he has loved. I don't care how much into loving women he may be about. And I feel that women, just in general, have an innate resentment of the role they are born into in man's society, and this has nothing to do with what is now known as women's liberation. I just think they can't help it.

"No matter how close a man and a woman become in a relationship, there are areas of themselves that never get explored. A man can never be as sensitive to a woman's needs and feelings as another woman can be to a woman's needs and feelings, because a man just doesn't come from that background. He's not a woman. Plus he has spent all of his life sublimating all of the things that are of an emotional nature similar to the emotional nature of a woman—his sensitivity, his ability to really express himself emotionally, tears, anger, what have you. Only if it's a masculine expression will he give vent to it.

"And most women suffer so much, just being women, in this society, that they have very limited sympathies for the plight of men. They will listen for a while, but then something in them naturally says, 'What about my pain? I know you've been through a lot, but what about what I've been through?' I think this is especially true of black women."

"So we've come to the same point in history but have traveled different roads to get here."

"Yes. I have a great deal of love for women, too. I guess I just love to give myself to whoever I relate to on any level. I make a sharp separation between love and sex. I love only men, but I can have sex with anything, and I do have sex with whatever I have a hunger for, man or woman. That's why I hate the word bisexual. I just like to say I'm open to receive human vibrations from any source from which they come. Now, you can't tell me that any man who opens himself up to a man he likes couldn't go the extra step and have sex with that man.

"Since I've lived in New York, I have always lived in duplex apartments because I don't like doing anything on just one level. You just can't let yourself go through life in one pair of shoes. There are so many styles and colors."

"Is anyone else in your family gay?"

"No. My father is a professor at one of the black schools in North Carolina. I don't think he's gay, but I've always had my doubts. He was a big-time athelete in college and he still has all these meetings and rah-rah rallies with the fellows who were on various teams with him. Even if they don't get down to homosexual acts, what is that but homosexual attraction? They just cut it off at a point, at a very unnatural point.

"When I was coming up, everyone used to say that I was just like him. My aunt and uncle, especially, used to say that we were just alike. So I began thinking: If I am like him, then he is like me, and if he is like me, then da-da-da-dum." He laughs.

"I realized I was gay at a very early age. I had my first experience with a male when I was ten years old. That was my first experience of a sexual nature with anyone. It happened with a little boy who was only eight but he knew what to do."

"Did you enjoy it?"

"Yes."

"When did you have your first sexual experience with a woman?"

"At seventeen."

"Did you enjoy it?"

"Yes, but I spent my entire teen-age years trying to be exclusively homosexual. That was my greatest ambition, but I always enjoyed the company of girls, so I would get involved with a girl on some level or other and end up making love to her. Being intellectuals, my parents were very open-minded. I was always encouraged to express myself in whatever way I wanted to. I took them to task for that and went ahead and did it. I used to have sex right in my home with my mother in another room doing housework or having a teachers' meeting.

"I usually made love to the girls downstairs in the living room and reserved the upstairs for the boys." He laughs and leans back in his chair. "I guess during that time I had more relationships with girls than with boys but I had this burning desire to be exclusively homosexual. I had a fairly active sex life in college in New York. That's how I came to New York.

"I went to Columbia University to train to be a credit to society, but by the time I had gotten out of school I had been so spoiled by men and women that I didn't feel that I had to work. I was selling my body, selling my warmth, my sympathy and understanding. I was being taken care of very well, by white and black men and women. I still sell my body sometimes."

"To mostly men or women?"

"No man would pay for me," Cecil smiled. "One look and he'd know that he could have me for free. Women buy me things. Let's put it that way. I buy them things, but I always make sure they buy me more than I buy for them. My wife supports us on a day-to-day basis, but then I make money as a disco DJ. I come home with something expensive for her. . . . I shouldn't admit it but I will. I play the same kinds of games that other men play. One thing I do is use my homosexuality to get over with women. It's a fallacy to believe that by being a he-man you'll get more women. Gay men get more women than a so-called straight man ever can. Women trust me. They feel safe with me. Their husbands or boy friends allow them to be with me.

"Women take me into their confidence. 'Oh, he's a faggot, we don't have to worry about him.' But before they know it they find me into their middles, front or rear.

"I think I am more successful sexually with women. I am more satisfying sexually to women. Men are such role-players. They have their own set of expectations. Love-making must start off this way and then it must move to this and then we do this.

"Women don't have a set of expectations. They are willing to let it happen like it happens. They are ready to respond to whatever is offered. Men make me sick, but I am more satisfied sexually with a man. It's a different kind of involvement. I never compare the two as an either-or situation. When I'm hungry for steak, I order steak. When I'm hungry for chicken, I order chicken.

"And I don't make substitutions. When I want a man I go after a man. A lot of men, and women too—people in general —are into fantasizing, and you know psychologists say that this is perfectly all right. You know you're together and you're imagining that she is not who she is and she's imagining that you're someone other than who you are. She's imagining that you're King Kong or Superfly. And they say this is fine if it helps your relationship, but I say it's not fine because it's not real. If you want King Kong you should go out and find King Kong.

"And if you're a man being with a woman, fantasizing that you're with a man, you should be honest enough to go out and find a man. Don't take substitutions. Don't have her sticking her finger or a knotted handerkerchief or beads up your rectum. Try the real thing if it's nothing more than a laboratory experiment. . . . It all makes me so ill."

"Tough being free, loving free, huh?"

"Toughest thing in the world."

"By the way, what is love?"

"Uh-h-h, what is love?" He pauses for a long time. "Love is being able to totally accept yourself, with all of your limitations, shortcomings, as well as whatever you feel that is positive about yourself; and then being able to transfer that acceptance to another person—being able to accept them as you accept yourself."

"You love your present lover?"

"With all my heart and soul."

"You love your wife?"

"Yes."

"She love you?"

"Yes."

"Your lover love you?"

He pauses for a moment. "You rat!"

"You see the contradiction? He can't love if he doesn't accept himself."

"Yes, but he does accept himself fully in a way. Anyway, love is always a state of becoming. You're always searching for complete love but you never find it. He's still struggling to find love, just as I am," Cecil gets up and goes to the door of the control booth. "He may not be coming tonight. He has a whole fleet of gypsy cabs to keep on the street."

"Is your wife gay?"

"No, but I think she should be."

"Why?"

"It would make her a better, rounded person, but she claims she can't get into that."

"But she wishes you happiness?"

"She wishes me dead."

I laugh at this sudden turn of the conversation. Is he joking?

"No, she loves me, but she wishes me dead so she wouldn't have to worry about losing me."

"Is there a danger?"

"There's always the danger. I might go out here tonight and a giant bald eagle will swoop down and carry me off."

"Why would the eagle want to do that?"

"Who knows? Who ever knows about anything? It wouldn't be surprising if the eagle happened to like gays," he says.

"Nor would it be surprising if the eagle happened not to like them," I say.

He laughs.

18

Girl in the Chinese Restaurant

I've never really had time to be in love. . . .

I knew there was something, but the first one to identify it, to pin it down for me, was the Chinese waiter at the Hong Kong Garden Restaurant. I had been going to Chinese restaurants for more than twenty years and Chinese waiters always seemed rather nonchalant people who go about doing their jobs as graciously and inconspicuously as possible. But it was the waiter in the Hong Kong Garden who went out of his way to point it out.

He was not even our waiter, but he came over after she had gotten up to go to the ladies' room. He held fingers spread, pointing to his own two eyes. "Her eyes," he said. "Her eyes, ver'li beautiful eyes. She's a ver-li beautiful girl," and he and our waiter began discussing her beauty in hushed tones of awe containing a mixture of Chinese and English.

It was her eyes, I suddenly knew. I had noticed when I first saw her that she was more than just a beautiful woman, but I hadn't put my finger on the single feature that made her stand out in New York, a city of beautiful women. It was the eyes. She had the most haunted eyes—big, penetrating, glossy, and a little cruel. Eyes so unusual that they could blow a Chinese waiter's mind.

She came back to the table smiling. This was the third interview I was having with her. The food came—big pink shrimps in a sauce with green squash and mushrooms and peppers. She spooned rice onto her plate from a small, flowered bowl, then covered the rice with scallops and snow-pea pods. On the side she put strips of roast pork so reddish that they seemed to contain food coloring. The shrimps and squash came last. She leaned over and let the aroma come up into her face.

I wondered what it was like to have to live your entire life with people stealing glances at you, or staring at you, or nudging their companion so the companion wouldn't miss your passing, so they could comment on your looks after you were gone. I wondered what it was like to have eyes like Sylvia's.

Sylvia hadn't eaten at restaurants all that often. She had never been part of the New York society that eats at fine restaurants three or four times a week. She was the kind who'd think that such practices were wasteful. "Think of all the good things you could buy with that money."

She thought that this was an expensive restaurant, but few Chinese restaurants are expensive when compared to the usual rates in New York City.

Her black hair glowed. Too much makeup on her cheeks gave her brown skin an artificial blush. "I've never had the time to be in love," she said.

The waiter came past the table leading a young couple toward a booth in the back. He looked at her, smiling. The young couple looked. There was just a little too much red on her lips. Her real eyelashes had been thickened. They made her eyes look even more flashy than they were. "It takes time to be in love," she said. "I wish I had a chance to feel all of those things, but I've never had that chance."

"I married for security reasons," she said. "My husband knew I didn't love him. He took the chance that I could learn to love him. In fact, he said just that: 'Maybe you could learn to love me, baby, and if you don't, I love you enough for both of us. I want to marry you anyway,'" she said, eating slowly, not being at all dramatic or emotional. There was a flat matter-of-factness in her voice.

"I was desperate," she said. "My mother, she wasn't going to take me back. I was sixteen. I had dropped out of high school and here I was sixteen, with this man thirty-seven who owned a house, who had a car, who had everything. He had a bank account and nice furniture. He had other property. It was all there. It was all laid out for me, and he was begging me to take it. I told him I didn't love him," she said and ate a big forkful of scallops and snow-pea pods.

It was easy to see why he would want to own her. She was lovely now, at twenty-three. At sixteen there must have been something even more strange and hungry in her eyes, and considering what her appearance suggested about her sexuality, and what her words later confirmed, it was not surprising that he would want to marry her anyway, to bring her into his unspectacular life, to make a fair trade with her. He would support her well. She wouldn't have to do a thing; in return all she had to do was light up his life, give him one glimmering something in the workaday world.

"That's what happens to beautiful girls," I said.

"I don't think I'm beautiful," she said. I knew enough to know that there is not a beautiful woman anywhere on earth who doesn't know she is beautiful. "He said he wanted to take care of me. He did want to take care of me."

That, I had no reason to doubt; but, even though he might not have known it, his urge to protect must have been tainted by less selfless motives, tainted by something that he wanted to own in her huge eyes.

"I wasn't particularly large or mature for my age. I had been doing some modeling, photographic modeling as a girl," she said. "People would just come up to me on the street and ask could they take my picture, mostly of my face.

"I met my husband on the street. I had just been assaulted. Assaulted is not the right word. Raped. I had just been raped, but I don't like to talk about that much because it still bothers me. Four guys raped me and I stumbled out of this alley and he was there. He had heard some scuffling in the alley. I was ashamed. I convinced him not to call the police. So what could he do but take me home? What could I do but go? My mother had said she didn't want to see me again.

"I went to his house in the Bronx but I wouldn't tell him anything about me, so he had no way of locating my folks. I made him promise not to call the police. I begged him.

"So it was a thing where actually no one was to blame. I wasn't trying to take advantage of him. I was just scared. He didn't make any demands on me, but I thought it was right if I stayed at his home for free that I give him some loving. He didn't want much. It was worth the trade to have somewhere to stay. I just didn't want to be out in the streets again. Ever since I was ten, you don't know how men have looked at me," she said.

"And you say you don't know that you're beautiful?" I asked.

"Well, when I was young I had huge eyes in a tiny face.

Girl in the Chinese Restaurant   245

That made people stare at me. I had a Twiggy kind of appeal."

"Yea, Twiggy," I said.

She didn't seem to know that I was teasing her, that with breasts like hers she never could have had a Twiggy appeal. She was a serious, single-minded woman who didn't respond to little quips. She kept on with her line of talk: "I left home when I was thirteen because I couldn't stand my stepfather, who wasn't really my legal stepfather. He and my mother weren't married but I called him my stepfather because he had been living with us ever since my real father got killed in the Korean War.

"He was my mother's boy friend and he was a policeman and he used to get drunk and he walked around the apartment with his gun out, pointing it at us. And my brother, who was bigger than I was, would try to make him stop and he would stomp my brother into the floor.

"And then when my mother got home she was so hung up on the guy she wouldn't believe us. She would believe him. She would believe that we were just making up stuff. He used to get off on that. Calvin Grant was his name. He would get high, pull out his gun, and say, 'Everybody get in bed.' Sometimes he would click the gun. He thought it was funny, but that gun coulda gone off any night. Maybe then my mother woulda believed us.

"I left, and went to live with this wealthy white woman on Park Avenue. I had seen her ad in the newspaper for someone to take care of her two kids. She requested a college student but I didn't care, I was desperate. It was a thing where I explained to her and I cried. She really saw how desperate I was.

"So she took a whole month off work and taught me how to handle the kids. She was a writer, and her husband was an architect. They had a huge apartment. I got fifty dollars a week, a room of my own, and they paid my tuition to a private girls' school.

"I liked it there. Her kids really dug me. I love to cook and the kids loved my scrambled eggs and down-home biscuits.

246   *Love, Black Love*

They didn't want the regular cook around for breakfast. I cooked for the kids and we all went off to school. There weren't that many black kids in the school where I was going, and it used to bother me if any of the white girls from my school saw me in the park nursemaiding these two little white kids. I would feel funny, because none of them knew I was a nursemaid, and they would see me in the park attending these little white kids and they'd say, "Oh!"

"As more and more of them found out, I started staying away from school more and more, and whereas my grades all along had been pretty good, I started flunking things.

"And when I took the two kids to the park or walking along Fifth Avenue and I'd call to them and they wouldn't come and I had to yell at them, I felt that every white person in the park was looking at me, saying, 'What's she doing yelling at those kids like that?' People never said anything, but there's a look they can give you. So I quit that job. I went to live with my cousin up on 138th Street. Funny thing is, I was in the park about four years ago and I saw this woman looking at me and she said, 'Don't I know you?' And it was the same woman. She had always liked me and she wanted me to stay in touch. I have her phone number. I called her when I was breaking up with my husband.

"She told me I could stay at their summer house on Long Island, but I didn't want to. I didn't, I don't want to keep being in a necessity bag. When I call her next time, I don't want it to be a necessity thing. Because I've always gotten myself into a necessity trap and someone always bailed me out," she said.

That was easy to explain, too, I thought, watching her, because there was something missing in her logic. All the steps were not there in her line of reasoning toward what she wanted. Something she said made you think she had the instincts of a street fighter, but she was naïve in certain very important ways. There was no doubt that she wanted to move up in class. That was revealed in the curious habit she had of calling all men "gentlemen," these workaday men who could offer her little more than protection and consumer goods that they would have to buy on credit and pinch to pay monthly notes on.

They were more than willing to do for her, but there was very little they could afford to do, and when they had done their best they found it hard to understand why she did not accept it as enough. Like the man who tried to kill himself because she wanted to leave him.

She had lived with him for five months. He had said it was okay. He wouldn't bother her sexually. He would support her. He would sit on the side of the bed and look at her. He would ask her if there was anything she wanted. He would go out in a rainstorm to get it.

She was in the process of leaving him when she came home one day and found he had taken an overdose of sleeping pills. She had to wait in the hospital three hours to know if he was going to live or die.

"He couldn't support me," she said. "It wouldn't have been right taking the little bit of money he had. He tried to give me nice things. He would have gotten a second job to give me the things he wanted me to have. I only have a few things, but I have very nice things. I feel like a man should be able to give me things without putting himself in a bind."

She was talking about men with discretionary income of greater magnitude than any of the men she met. A man had given her two $400 dogs as sleek and elegant as she was. They were Fifth Avenue dogs that lived with her in the Bronx. She had a $1,300 mirrored sleeping cube wired for stereo sound in an apartment that was one step above a project. Such were the contradictions of her life.

She had survived in the meanest streets. Yet she knew very little about the streets. How could she? She had been married when she was sixteen and under the protection of rich white people for two years before that.

Now, at twenty-three, she was in a hurry, dating fast. She had a daughter, and if nothing else, she would want her daughter to grow to be a lady dating men with discretionary incomes in the five-figure magnitude.

But she worried that she didn't stay home with her daughter much. Other people kept her daughter for her a lot. She worried about that, but she was too much in a hurry to stay home and be just a mother. How could she meet love by doing that? And her daughter had seen some ugly things that she wished never for her daughter to have to see.

"I was on the bus the other day and my daughter saw some scratches on my hand, and she asked, 'Did John do that to you, Momma?'" John is the man who tried to kill her. "'Is that where John hit you?' My daughter knew. My daughter knew even though she didn't see the fight. It affected her."

There were no scars on Sylvia's face. It was smooth. The skin shone. She said she is the kind of energetic woman who burns up fat, leaving herself always thin no matter how much she eats. She is not thin so much as narrow. "There's a three-thousand-dollar red fox coat I want and I'm gonna get it if it's the last thing I do," she said. She probably will get it within a year. Someone will give it to her and she'll not understand why that man insists on owning her in return, why he might try to croak her if she gets the coat and decides to move on. Like the man who took her out of a shabby hotel on the Grand Concourse where she was living with her daughter shortly after she moved away from the guy who tried to kill himself. This guy met her, found out where she was living, and convinced her that she didn't have to live there, that it was bad for herself and her daughter. He said she could come and live with him. In about two weeks he fell in love with her, "Because of the way I treat a man," she says. "When I make love to a man, I don't think of myself. I think about him first and foremost and I'm willing to do anything he wants me to do.

"He said he was in love with me. He wanted us to get married. I told him I wanted to be sure." While he was waiting for her to be sure, he gave her things. He bought her a twenty-five-inch Zenith color television trying to help her to make up her mind. He bought her a stereo. It was he who bought her the $1,300 mirrored, wired-for-sound, modular sleeping cube. He bought a bedroom set for her child, clothes.

She liked him but she did take a long time to make up her mind that she would probably never love him.

"How come you won't marry me?" he yelled. He called her the vilest names he could think of. The last time she saw him was in the street, with his hands around her neck trying to choke her to death.

"John, you're killing me. John, I can't breathe.

"Even though it's never happened to me, I believe in love. I would like very much to be in love. I want a lot of children, but unfortunately children cost money. I'd like to have eleven boys and one girl. I would like to shape that girl into a dynamite lady, and all of her brothers would be around to make her feel like a queen," she said.

"You have the royal instinct, then?" I said.

"At this point in my life I do like nice things. I see nice things and I don't see why I can't have them for myself. In my childhood and my marriage I did without so much. When Donald, my husband, started out, we had the things we needed but he was not interested in fancy things. I more or less conformed to his taste. I won't deny he did a lot for me. After I got raped he was very kind to me. I remember he bought each of us a ten-speed bike and we used to ride all over town. That was nice. In those days I could dig that as a form of love.

"I was the person who made him feel young. In fact, we rode our bikes down to get married. We were married by this gypsy woman who taught classes in astrology, meditation, and higher awareness, and it was known that she had ways of marrying people legally even though I was under age.

"It was nice. One of her astrology classes was our wedding ceremony. The class stood up and they seemed so happy that we were married. That blew my head.

"Donald was already into meditation, yoga, and vegetarianism, and after we got married he got me into that. I have a very open mind and so I started reading all those books on higher states of awareness.

"We didn't have a honeymoon per se, but we rode all over town on our bicycles. I was happy then. Donald was happy.

He had never been married before, so his family was glad to see it at first. It was a thing like, 'Hey, you've finally brought home a woman.'

"I wanted to make the marriage work. I guess I worked harder at it because I felt guilty because I didn't love him. I really wanted it to be beautiful. I ordered a lot of sexy outfits. I ordered vibrators. I ordered sexual games. I dig things like that. I love sex. I love pleasing a man. I love giving myself. I tried to get into that with him, but he wouldn't. He had an uptight attitude. I had a little movie projector so we would dig some films even though most of the films were so bad, you see so much dick and ass that it doesn't do anything for you after a while, but then, too, there are a lot of things you see in a film that you might want to try, and you can have fun trying them. I don't know how I got like that. I hadn't had much experience, but it's not a matter of experience. I just had a very free mind and I think when you get behind closed doors you should be free to do whatever pleases you.

"It would have been good if I had hooked up with a man who wanted to act out his fantasies. I'm the kind who wants to do or be whatever you want me to be—not careerwise, that has to be me by myself, but as far as being your woman. If you want me to dress up as a nurse then I'll do that. I'm open to so many things as long as it doesn't involve group sex or violence. As long as it involves the softer tones of love.

"But my husband wouldn't please me and he wouldn't let me please him. He thought of it all as something nasty. About a year after we were married, I got pregnant and my husband got deeper and deeper into yoga and vegetarianism and all these health books like this book *You Can Live Forever.*

"He really got freaked out on these books. One book would tell him to do one thing and another would tell him something else. His goal was to live forever. He felt that man was not born to die. He said that he was going to become like a little child again.

"We exercised together and we fasted. One time I fasted for twenty-five days, only taking juices—carrot juice and spinach juice. It's easy. The first three days are the worst. After the third day your body adjusts. But one time he fasted for sixty days. He fainted.

"It was blowing my mind seeing him like that—skinny, his veins all popping out. He would go out on the terrace and exercise and fall asleep out there, and there I'd be in bed alone.

"That's when I started talking about leaving, but I still wanted to communicate, to talk about it to make the relationship better, but he wouldn't talk. He was obsessed with this idea of cleansing his body and his mind so he could live forever.

"The Yogi Gupta would say that a human being could live on one bean sprout a day. Donald, my husband, would believe him. But what used to freak my mind is that the Yogi Gupta was a big fat man, and there's no way that man could be living on one bean sprout.

"In yoga they have this thing where you can stick a handkerchief up one nostril and pull it out the other. It's very difficult to do, but Donald could do it. He was really gone on this stuff. All he thought about was yoga. His hair started coming out and stuff, and I kept saying, 'Look at yourself. Look at yourself.' His face started hanging.

"Then he wanted the kid to eat as he ate—salads in the mornings. No hot cereal. That was our total life. I started working as a model to make some money, because this health food is expensive. He wanted the baby to have goat's milk. A dollar and a quarter for a little container and he had to have five of those a week. And Donald would buy a whole case of carrots to make into juice, and a whole case of nuts. We were always broke and I had to sneak over to a friend's house in order to feed the baby regular food.

"I kept saying, 'We aren't getting anywhere. This isn't getting us anywhere.' We sat home night after night, and I would tell him that he wasn't satisfying me, and he would say, 'Why don't you find somebody else?'

"I would say, 'You keep saying that, Donald, and one day I will.' So after a while, I did. I went out, not for sexual satisfaction but for the fun of being out. No sex was involved, because I knew if I started getting sexual satisfaction outside the home I would stop trying at home.

"I went out with a lot of gentlemen, to the movies, to a show or a club. It was a new experience for me, because I got married at sixteen and I didn't have a chance to do all this.

"But then I found out that if a gentleman takes you out, he usually wants you to go to bed with him. I've always carried myself as a lady, but men always thought if they spent a lot of money on you, you should be willing to go to bed with them.

"There was one time when this gentleman took me out and spent a great deal of money on me and after we got into the car he drove straight to the motel without asking. I said, 'Hey, wait a minute. We hadn't discussed a motel. It was supposed to be a dinner and a show.' He told me that it was understood that the motel was supposed to round out the evening, and if I didn't want to go to the motel then I had to give his money back.

"I can only love one man at a time, and if any other man made me feel good I thought that would be unfair to my husband.

"I wanted to keep on trying with my husband, but he wouldn't grow. He wouldn't share thoughts and ideas. I'm a very experimental person. I have no limits as far as sex is concerned.

"He didn't believe in anything like oral sex. People have hang-ups. They can't deal with licking you under the arms or screwing you in the butt. People cut off their bodies in different sections and place certain sections off limits, but I think there should be no end as long as the body is clean.

"That's something I could never understand about myself. I hadn't had much experience before I got married. Nobody taught me these things. I guess as a person that's the way I am.

"I always had these fantasies about how I wanted to be as a woman and how I wanted to love a man, and not exactly that he had to love me in the same way, but I want him to love me in his way, physically. I wouldn't want him to think of certain things that I wanted to do or that he wanted to do as nasty.

"Like, when I'm making love I talk. I moan and groan and talk. I like to say a lot of things that people call nasty things, if you want to use that term, but I don't consider it nasty. It turns me on and I've found that it turns some gentlemen on. When I get in bed I just like to get nasty, so to speak.

"So for a long time I had it in my mind that I would have to leave Donald. I was looking for love, but then there was the necessity thing again. I didn't have the time or money to wait for the right person. I had to find a place for me and my daughter to stay, so I had to forget about love and deal with necessity.

"Maybe there's no such thing as love, but I still hope that there is. It gives me something to work for even if I never find perfect love. When you give up trying, you get very lonely. It's one thing to be alone, but it's much worse to be lonely while you're with someone. Like, when you want to cry if you're alone, you can cry. When someone is there with you, you can't even do that freely unless that someone loves you. I've never had that.

"It blows my mind to be lying in bed with someone who isn't really there; that's the way it's been with me and men. My husband finally got so bad that he thought that he could get all of his nourishment from the sun. He would go to the Botanical Gardens and sit in the sun for hours. He would sit out on the terrace for hours.

"I couldn't live with that. I had to leave, but just to show how funny life is, now that we've been separated for almost two years he eats his McDonald's hamburger and his pizza. He said he's changed. He wants me back more than ever. We talk. We try to communicate more than we ever did before. We've tried to get back together.

"We made love and we tried to do some of the things he had been inhibited from doing before, but I cried. I knew I could never go back with him. You can never go back in life. When we made love, I could tell how bad he wanted me back. That's why he did these things that he never would do before. He wanted me back that bad. That's why I broke down and cried. I felt sorry for him and I felt sorry for me, too. It made me begin to doubt myself for the first time. Would I ever find love."

T